What You Should Know About

Cybersecurity

What You Should Know About Cybersecurity

Dr. Mohammed Al-Dorani

Hamad Bin Khalifa University Press
P.O. Box 5825
Doha, Qatar

www.hbkupress.com

First English edition in 2022

ISBN: 9789927161070

Printed in Beirut-Lebanon

Qatar National Library Cataloging-in-Publication (CIP)

Al-Dorani, Mohammed, author.

What you should know about cybersecurity / Dr. Mohammed Al-Dorani. First English edition. – Doha, Qatar : Hamad Bin Khalifa University Press, 2022.

pages ; cm

ISBN 978-992-716-107-0

Includes bibliographical references (pages 159-163).

1. Computer networks -- Security measures. 2. Internet -- Security measures. 3. Data protection. 4. Consumer protection. 5. Cyberterrorism. I. Added title: Cybersecurity. II. Title.

TK5105.59. D67 2022
005.8 – dc 23

202228430074

Contents

INTRODUCTION

This book is an introduction to cybersecurity, intended to help the general public understand the importance of this ever-expanding field. The topic has become increasingly relevant as cyberattacks intensify around the globe.

The subject will be discussed in general terms, since the technologies, tools, policies and processes associated with cybersecurity have become increasingly complex. The average computer user is still baffled by the ability of hackers to take control of digital devices, such as laptops, iPads, mobile phones and the IoT ('Internet of Things'). In general, people do not understand what they have done wrong. It is even harder to explain to them how it happened. The majority shake their heads and consider cyberattacks to be irrelevant to their daily lives. They feel that they do not have any sensitive information stored in their devices relevant to hackers. The majority even believe that hackers and cyberattackers only target people in a sensitive position or those in government. For the average person, an attempt on their digital device to obtain information is not important, so ignorance plays a significant role in making the job of hackers easy.

The general public does not realize that all digital media, especially laptops and mobiles, contain personal information (documents, pictures, videos, email, text messages, etc.) which can be copied, transferred or stolen. Such private information can be used as a bargaining chip for ransom, threats, intimidation, fraud and other types of cybercrime. There are many cases of people falling prey to phishing emails and identification fraud which have caused them emotional and financial stress. Such valuable personal and financial information should be protected at all costs and by any means. Once they are out in cyberspace, no one can predict how those involved in organized crime and groups of hackers will utilize them criminally and illegally.

This book will shed light on various key subjects linked to cybersecurity and cybercrime, such as the multiple definitions and terminologies commonly used by the public, as well as standard technical terms, different cyber threats, password security, viruses and malware, email security, Internet security, computer security, physical security, wireless security, identity theft, social engineering, and backup and recovery.

As the topic of cybersecurity and cybercrime is vast and limitless, it will not be covered in depth. This book acts as an introduction to this broad topic and readers are encouraged to engage in further research, using the various references available in cyberspace.

Cybercrime is a daily threat to our way of life, both on a personal and a global scale. Current cyberattacks on various countries' infrastructures remind us all that without such foundations, our comfortable daily lifestyle cannot continue. Current technologies and the evolution of social media have enabled hackers of various types to threaten not only our freedom but also our everyday life as we know it.

Cybersecurity has become national security for all nations. It poses a threat to infrastructures, especially security and the military establishment. How nations are attacking other countries by utilizing their advanced cybersecurity tools is explored in this book, including the Stuxnet virus attack on Iranian nuclear facilities; attacks on water and electrical grids and networks; social media affecting elections and the media, such as the attack on the Qatar News Agency; attacks on financial systems and the disabling of various infrastructures in countries such as Estonia and the Ukraine. These examples will be highlighted to show readers the seriousness of cyberattacks, especially in smaller nations. Countries with advanced cybersecurity are fighting each other, utilizing the latest technological tools in their arsenals. Cyber espionage on security and military establishments is not only a daily occurrence, but it also happens at commercial and industrial sites across the world. Countries which do not have research and development (R&D) capabilities have resorted to cyber espionage to steal industrial blueprints and intellectual property, saving themselves from having to invest and spend millions of dollars on R&D.

Thus, cybersecurity has become an important topic amongst decision makers in government and the private sector. Cybercrime is ranked as the number one threat to businesses and protection must be provided at all costs. The subjects of cybersecurity and cybercrime have become more important, given the proliferation of identity fraud and email phishing, utilizing social engineering and social media applications. Hackers working either individually or with gangs have infiltrated users' accounts. They can access reports in multiple ways and post them for sale on the Dark Web. Many businesses realize their systems have been hacked after users' credentials are posted in cyberspace. Such accounts are then used to blackmail or ransom individuals and business entities across the globe. With various devices nowadays connected to the Internet, it has become easy for hackers to obtain passwords and security pins to launch attacks not only locally but internationally.

This book will touch on the above issues and attempt to educate readers about the danger of cybercrime and the security levels required to enhance the safety and integrity of their digital devices and systems.

CHAPTER 1
Cybersecurity and Cybercrime Terminology - Most Common Technical Terms

Five years ago, cybersecurity and cybercrime terminology were not familiar to the general public. However, since then, many users of digital devices have been harmed by hackers illegally accessing their private information and as a result, more people have become acquainted with them.

But still, when asked what cybersecurity is, many people understand it as a mixture of terms linked to security, the Internet, hacking, loss of data and others. There is no unified understanding of the definition of these essential terms and there is still confusion between information security and cybersecurity. Although the two terms are closely connected in their operations and with regards to safety, the public understands them to mean the security of physical computers and digital devices. It is essential for a novice to understand certain cybersecurity terms, which have become common in cyberattack incidents.

Here is a list of the most pertinent terminology relating to the field for the non-specialist reader.

Adware. The term is used generally to mean that certain viruses and worms are launched when an individual clicks on an advertisement appearing on a digital device. Most of these types of attacks use fake ads intended to launch malware into target systems. With the popularity of social media applications and the increasing flood of advertisements on Facebook, Instagram, Telegram, Twitter and the like, the number of people affected by adware is growing considerably.

Anti-Virus. This software system sold by cybersecurity companies and software developers is installed on digital devices to identify, prevent and clean devices of all viruses and worms. There are various levels of development with regards to capabilities, and the more advanced an anti-virus system is, the higher the cost, but it is essential as the first front line of defense.

APT (Advanced Persistent Threats). This is now a popular term that describes those hackers with advanced persistent capabilities. Nation states and criminal groups who possess advanced tools and hacking technologies are characterized as APT. When such a hacking has occurred, it is challenging to discover the source. Viruses and worms launched by APT can stay hidden for longer periods. APT hackers can cause severe damage to targeted assets.

Assets. Refers to targeted digital devices' assets in cyberattacks. They also represent victims' assets, whatever they may be.

Authentication. The process of ensuring that the owner of an account has the legal authority to access it and the account is not being accessed by an unknown individual. Authentication can be two-factor based on user identification and a password, or three-factor. In three-factor authentication, there is an additional level of security identification of the user. This might be a digital PIN or a series of private questions to individuals. There are also other advanced forms of authentication, such as biometric identification.

Authorization. Refers to the legal right of access into a system and specific applications. A user can be authorized to access the human resource module of the software system but not financial records — such authorization may be given by the network administrator or database manager.

Availability. Information transmitted, received, stored and retrieved should be available to the custodian/owner at all times. Compromising available data is a significant concern to decision makers dealing with cyberspace.

Backdoor. A term used in the cybersecurity world to mean the ability of hackers to install a worm capable of re-entering a network system and accounts.

Backup and Recovery. This is an essential activity for any organization, small or large, in addition to individuals. The process of backing up data in storage devices and also on the cloud is a necessary activity. Recovery must be possible in case of loss or deletion of data. There are several recovery tools available on the market.

Black Hat Hackers. This term defines hackers as "black hat" due to the illegal hacking in which they engage. They are extremely dangerous and work on penetrating computer systems and launching viruses and worms, inflicting severe damage.

Blockchain. A new technology of journaling/recording all transactions in blocks that are chained together. It provides efficiency, authenticity and security, utilizing various geographically distributed nodes/servers to enable the sustainability of its services. The term is a new one and not many people understand what it means. Due to its very technical nature, there is uncertainty as to its merit in helping general security to minimize cyberattacks. The benefits of implementing Blockchain technology across organizations' transactions have shown its great potential. However, when it comes to cybersecurity, the jury is still out, and we will have to see how this technology can protect transactions from cyberattacks.

Bot/Botnet. A compromised digital device used as a slave to send a flood of transactions and other types of malicious codes to an intended target. Owners of devices infected by malicious viruses and worms do not know that their digital tools have been taken over and utilized for launching attacks on websites and servers.

Breaches. Access and publication of material obtained from illegal exploiting of digital devices such as computers and mobile phones, utilizing malicious viruses and worms. Data breaches are increasing exponentially and many cases have been reported in recent years.

Brute Force Attack. This term applies to the technique used to crack a password key which cannot be broken by other means. Various tools, techniques, dictionaries and hashing passwords are used to match the wanted password of target victims. Brute Force is applied when passwords and security pins are encrypted and impossible to crack by any other methods. It may take longer to crack an encrypted password using Brute Force than to uncover standard unencrypted passwords.

Bug. Refers to an error discovered in a software code of a program or application. These bugs are similar to vulnerabilities and must be patched and upgraded urgently to avoid exploitation by hackers.

Cloud. Information services and technology provided by a third party utilizing telecommunications and the Internet. Software, hardware, storage, retrieval, security, and backup and recovery are all provided by a third party over the Internet at demand. The utilization of cloud technology is widespread, since it reduces cost and is efficient and effective in the storage and retrieval of information. Cyberattacks against stored data have occurred and there are cases reported of data breaches of cloud-stored data.

Command and Control Server. The server used to command and control other digital devices. Also, the term is applied to central command in military and intelligence operations whereby an operations room with a centralized computer system is set up to monitor, manipulate and control all traffic and transactions. Furthermore, hackers utilize this option to launch multiple attacks on several targets.

Confidentiality. An essential aspect of cybersecurity is to maintain confidentiality. It means that end-to-end communication and transmission of information should be confidential and not compromised by a third party. Privacy can involve secrecy and applying the latest technology and tools, involving encryption and cryptography.

Critical Infrastructure. This term refers to those forms of infrastructure which are critical to daily life. They include but are not limited to transportation, telecommunications, electrical and water grids, hospitals, education, military and intelligence, financial, banking and others. Cyberattacks aimed at such types of infrastructure can be devastating, since disabling any one of them can impact the daily life of citizens and cause severe human and economic damage. Nation states utilize advanced cyber tools and techniques to penetrate infrastructure during times of war.

Cryptography. The process of employing advanced encryption methods in transaction processing, whereby plain text is transformed into unreadable text. The use of private and public keys is necessary for applying cryptography. A well-known example is the use of cryptocurrency, where financial transactions become confidential and no third party can read the communications end-to-end. However, cryptography keys have been broken by skilled, persistent hackers.

Cross-Site Scripting (XSS). Insertion of a malicious code into a software system program that runs a website. These successful injections by hackers enable them to collect users' account information, such as IDs and passwords.

Cyberattacks. This term is a general one. It means an attack by hackers utilizing cyberspace, which is the Internet. Cyberattacks can come in many forms. The most common is the use of viruses and worms (Trojans) as a means to attack victims' digital devices. It is possible to recover from some cyberattacks, such as simple DoS/DDoS, but not from others, such as cyber espionage and terrorism.

Cyberattacks have become more frequent in recent years and will continue to multiply, given the nature of the malicious worms created, vulnerability (zero-day) discoveries, the advanced hacking tools utilized, the explosion of social media applications and widespread usage of mobile devices and the Internet of Things.

Cybercrime. This term consists of two words. Cyber is the World Wide Web (WWW), the Internet. Crime consists of illegal acts committed using recent technology over the Internet, such as identification fraud and theft, document counterfeits, online gambling, online pornography, stalking, bullying, skimming and many other types of cybercrime.

Cybersecurity. This term consists of two words. Cyber means the world of the Internet, or World Wide Web (WWW), while security is the ability to provide a secure line of communication where all types of data, including voice, messages, texts, files and other types of documents and social interactions using Internet applications are secure end-to-end between recipient and transmitter. Security also involves the integrity and confidentiality of communications on the Internet.

Cyber Espionage. Spying and collecting intelligence, whether political, economic or social, has become the work of nations and industrial corporations. Utilizing the Internet, hacking and worms have made cyber espionage famous. It is a challenge to uncover espionage worms as they have sophisticated capabilities which enable them to stay hidden in network systems.

Dark Web. There are multiple sites on the World Wide Web (WWW) which provide high security and confidentiality for members to share, exchange and transact without fear from the authorities, since these dark web sites have high encryption and privacy capabilities. Most of these sites operate underground and are considered illegal by many governments.

Data Mining. The process of utilizing mass data for analysis and decision making. Big companies which place vast quantities of data on individuals, groups of people and countries in large storage devices can mine such data for political, economic and social purposes. Currently, there is extensive usage of artificial intelligence (AI) tools and techniques to sniff out the required data for various purposes. With social media applications and data communication happening over the Internet, extensive data collection can be both beneficial and harmful. For example, Amazon and Facebook, two of the largest companies in the world, collect the data of over two billion people. Imagine the power of such information to these companies and others.

Digital Certificate. A certificate given to each individual owner of a digital device or software program. For example, if an individual purchases a laptop with an operating system, then a digital certificate is issued digitally. If an update, upgrade or change occurs in such an operating system, a digital certificate number must be utilized to ensure the authorization and integrity of users.

Domain. This is the authorized legal and regionally registered name for the account of a service/technology provider on the Internet. The name is unique and will have a website, multiple emails and IP addresses. Cloned domain names are easy to generate, using the creative means of domain names registration. When domain names are cloned and sent to victims, it is then easy to obtain all their private information, including passwords.

DoS/DDoS. Denial of Service/Distributed Denial of Service are the two terms used for a single attack or multiple distributed attacks. It is the use of bots/zombie digital devices, such as hacked computers and mobile units, to attack a target by flooding it with millions of transactions, disabling the target's network system due to the system's limited capabilities to process such a flood of transactions. In a DDoS attack, the Command and Control Server (C&C) is used to control all the highjacked bots/zombie units in order to launch an attack on a specific target or multiple targets.

End-to-End Encryption. This means that any communication or transactions using Internet applications and various social media apps are encrypted. However, many such applications have encryption capabilities and algorithms which are easy to break and compromise. Specific private end-to-end communication utilizes more advanced encryption algorithms which are harder to break.

Exploit. Hackers utilize various technological tools and malicious codes to penetrate computers and digital devices. They will look for vulnerabilities, especially zero-day vulnerabilities, creating the necessary codes and programs to infiltrate computer network systems.

Firewall. Hardware and software technology used to prevent any malicious activity from penetrating computer networks. It is a must-have technology to protect network systems from hacking and spam messages. Large and medium-sized organizations have implemented firewalls, along with anti-viruses, to protect their computing operations from cyberattacks. Small organizations with limited budgets which cannot afford to implement firewalls are most vulnerable to cyberattacks.

FTP/FTPS (File Transfer Protocol). This protocol allows digital devices such as computers and mobiles to transfer files and texts over the Internet. When data packets are moved across a network system, they should be protected by the FTP protocol but unfortunately this is not a secure type of data transmission, since FTP is unreliable and data acquired is read in plain text mode, while FTPS data packets are encrypted in a secure method of transmission.

Gateway. This hardware and software unit is necessary for any communication over the Internet. It is a network system connected to an Internet service provider which provides gateway access to the World Wide Web (WWW).

Hacker. A person skilled in information technology who uses their technical knowledge to achieve a goal or overcome an obstacle, within a computerized system by non-standard means.

Hacktivists. These are hackers who serve a specific agenda which is more political than economic. Their attacks can be harmless or cause damage, depending on their intentions. Some attacks are used for political and public awareness purposes.

Handshake Procedures. A procedure used frequently in identifying senders and receivers. It is used when a sender sends a request of communication to a receiver and acknowledgment must be returned to the sender, whereby the authenticity of the receiver is validated, and an exchange of transactions and transmission of files can commence. In a WiFi environment, three such handshakes are common, and hackers can intercept a handshake by acquiring the critical password of the sender.

Hashing. A technique used to transform plain text into unknown alphanumeric text that is difficult to read. It is an encryption technique that has become popular for disguising passwords and documents considered confidential. The use of passwords and keys is necessary to transform the hashed text into the original readable text.

Honeypot. A term used when authorities trap illegal operators by pretending that the sender is an authorized person. Victims or targeted individuals fall into the trap, not knowing that a honeypot has been set up to draw them into conversation or communication with the sender. Illegal actions are then recorded and monitored, and the lawful authority can take further action against criminals.

HTTP/HTTPS (Hypertext Transfer Protocol). This is one of the most common letters you will see when you surf the Internet. The only difference between HTTP and HTTPS is the letter s. Communication with a website linked to HTTPS is secured and all transactions on that site are encrypted. Hackers can read in plain text all communications with HTTP, but with HTTPS, they would need to use decryption algorithms to decipher the encrypted documents.

Identity Fraud. Refers to accessing, obtaining and using the identity of valid individuals illegally. With the advancements in hacking tools and techniques, a huge amount of such activity has taken place globally, with devastating impact on the lives of many people.

Identity Theft. Obtaining the identity of a valid individual. It results in criminal activity to defraud the targeted individual, by faking documentation, stealing money and/or acquiring their identity for illegal purposes. This practice has become widespread with the development of hacking tools and popularity of the Internet and social media.

IDS (Intrusion Detection Systems). These have become necessary prevention and identification tools used against cyber-attacks. They are advanced, expensive tools, but are essential to minimize the risk of attacks over the Internet. Given the advanced nature of their operations and cost, a large organization can afford to use them and provide the maximum cybersecurity needed. However, medium and smaller organizations which cannot afford to implement such systems are vulnerable to cyberattacks.

Inside Attacks. An inside job, an attack within an organization. These attacks are either made by individuals working physically inside the organization or by those who have physical access to the organization's computers and network systems.

Integrity. This involves the authenticity of data transmitted through Internet technology used in the delivery, utilization and storage of all types of information.

IP Address. Internet Protocol with a numeric address allowing transmission of information between two parties on the Internet. These addresses are unique when an Internet connection is established, securing delivery of data point-to-point. An IP address is considered the identity address of the sender of data to endpoint recipients. IP addresses belong to an authorized domain name.

IP Spoofing. The term "spoofing" means acquiring and obtaining an IP (Internet Protocol) of a valid user interacting over the Internet. The process involves obtaining the victim's IP (Internet Address Protocol) over the communication medium used to transmit data packets between the sender and receiver. There are multiple tools utilized by hackers to acquire IP addresses, which result in their being used for illegal purposes.

IPS (Intrusion Prevention System). This system utilizes advanced intrusion and prevention tools to stop viruses and worms attacking network systems. They can be very expensive but are necessary. Large organizations with the necessary funds have utilized them extensively, thereby reducing cyberattacks to a minimum.

ISP (Internet Service Provider). Refers to those companies authorized to offer Internet facilities to individuals, companies and the public sector. They are typically the telecommunications companies operating within a country, with a license. They provide the necessary gateway of hardware, software and system set-up to link computers, digital devices and networks to the World Wide Web (the Internet).

Keyloggers. This term means that all critical strokes made by users utilizing digital devices are logged. Hackers use tools to log users' keystrokes and they can then be read in plain text. It is a popular method of acquiring users' user identification, passwords and other types of information. Legal authorities utilize keylogger software system tools to record and retrieve all kinds of information about users.

LAN/WAN: Local Area Network/Wide Area Network. The first refers to a local area of networks for a specific organization located in one physical space. The second relates to a network area that is distributed across geographical regions but is interconnected.

Malware. This is a group of viruses and worms used by hackers to inflict damage on an existing network system. The malware is a malicious code with a specific task, depending on the agenda of the sender.

Man-in-the-Middle (MITM). Hackers who have access to the telecommunication system linking senders and receivers and intercept communication transactions. MITM hackers can collect, store and manipulate transferred information without the knowledge of senders and receivers. They are considered to be advanced and are able to target specific senders and receivers, utilizing the latest cyber tools and techniques.

Mobile Banking Trojan. The worm Trojan is used to steal banking credentials such as user identification, passwords, and other types of log-on security. It is very common to steal pins. Almost all banking applications provided to banks' customers require them to log on from either laptops or mobile devices. Hackers utilize weaknesses in these applications, either by cloning them or finding vulnerabilities in them, causing victims to log into fake websites of banks, believing they are the original. Having access to online access credentials means that personal banking information is exposed, and accounts are threatened by significant financial fraud.

Open WiFi vs. Encrypted. Every digital device has features of security used when transferring files and in exchanges of information. Open means that data transmitted is not encrypted and hackers can access information recorded in plain text. Encrypted means that the information transmitted is transferred from plain text into an unreadable format. There are multiple encryption options, such as WEP, WPA and WPA2. WEP has the lowest level of encryption and hackers have managed to break it, while others can be broken but require sophisticated hacking methods and tools.

Password Sniffing. The acquiring of a password while communication is taking place between two parties. Popular hacking tools are used for this. It is the most popular activity amongst hackers, since a password is considered the most valuable piece of information one can acquire in order to compromise users' accounts.

Patch & Updates. These are published and sent by manufacturers and software developers to clients whenever a vulnerability or weakness is detected, or an upgrade needed on the supplied software systems. This process of patching and upgrading is necessary to minimize any weaknesses that hackers could exploit.

This has been frequently ignored in the past. However, awareness of cyberattacks has raised the profile of this process.

Payment Card Skimmers. These are used in ATM machines, and "skimmers" refers to a process whereby a hardware device is used to collect credit and ATM banking card information stored on a magnetic stripe or chip.

Phishing/Spear Phishing. This is similar to fishing. The term "phis" indicates the collection of a vulnerable user's credentials, such as user identification and any other related security passwords. Spear phishing is more of a targeted approach, whereby a hacker will look for a specific target to attack. Both terms are very common, since this method of hacking has become widespread.

PKI (Public Key Infrastructure). The term refers to a key given to an individual and used publicly (i.e. shared with others) to conduct confidential and secure transactions. The key is required to encrypt and decrypt text sent and received between two parties.

Ransomware. A malicious worm delivered to a recipient by a hacker. Its objective is to disable the digital device and deny access to it and all stored files unless a ransom is paid by digital currency. When payment is made, a key is sent to the victim to restore access to the digital device. Since substantial financial rewards can be gained through using ransomware worms, malicious actors have launched them across the globe. Recovery is only possible if victims comply; otherwise, all access to digital devices is blocked by encryption. Rates of ransomware attacks are sure to increase as malicious actors find new and creative methods to launch attacks.

RAT (Remote Access Trojan). This refers to access by hackers remotely into digital devices such as computers and mobiles. The network system can provide remote access to users not just locally but internationally. This practice has been a threat and source of vulnerability to many organizations, and many have stopped allowing it or have limited it to specific individuals. Hackers can obtain authorized remote access via users' credentials and hack into network systems and servers, deliberately causing significant damage.

Reverse Engineering. To reverse a worm code to understand its content. The reverse engineer must have high technical coding skills to be able to reverse worm codes and discover types of viruses and worms. Furthermore, professional hackers are also able to discover vulnerabilities in a software system by conducting reverse engineering, thus developing malicious codes to launch in cyberattacks.

Rootkit. The bottom of the files. Files that are critical and sit in places which are hidden. They are essential to protect all other forms of data. Hackers typically target these rootkit files and hide their worms there.

SCADA. This term stands for Supervisory Control and Data Acquisition. This software system is used in different kinds of industrial environments. It utilizes and interconnects various devices that log and control data, such as the programmable logic controller PLC. It has a graphic interface to make it easier for a plant operator to monitor operations and ensure that all levels of communication and interface are operating normally. Although it is challenging to hack into industrial switches running the SCADA system, skilled and persistent hackers have managed to exploit its vulnerabilities.

Shoulder Surfing. This is a process used in social engineering. An old and new human technique whereby a smart, skilled individual can watch a target entering his or her credentials into a device, unaware that someone is watching over their shoulder.

Site Cloning (Farming). The copying and faking of original websites by hackers and criminal groups, using commercially available tools or ones created by them. Hackers send these cloned sites to victims using email systems or social media applications with invitation messages requesting them to click on or open files containing multimedia presentations. When a link has been clicked or a file opened, the cloned site appears, requesting online logging in information. This personal logging in information is then used by hackers to access accounts and applications of victims.

Sniffing. The word is associated with smelling or finding something. Hackers typically use specific sniffing tools that are either commercially available or created by them. The objective is to sniff all the data packets (transmitted information), looking for particular data, specific credentials such as user identification, passwords and other relevant information which can enable hackers to access victims' applications and accounts. Given the popular usage of mobile digital devices and apps, most sniffing is carried out in a WiFi environment.

SPAM. The term used when a large number of text messages are sent to a digital device that is not fully source identified. Anti-viruses and ISP systems can identify such a flood of transactions and transfer them into a SPAM account for further processing. They can be damaging to the network system because they use processing power and can jam a system.

Spyware. Refers to a worm launched by a hacker into a computer network. This spyware worm can stay undetected or in a state of stealth. It can collect and transfer any types of data stored or transacted on the digital device. It is used by nation states and spy agencies.

SQL Injection. This means that a hacker is able to inject a malicious code into the Sequential Query Language (SQL) used in a database. By inserting malicious codes, hackers can then direct and instruct the database to follow the new code commands, either by transferring or deleting existing material or injecting new unwanted material, etc.

Trojan Horse. A camouflaged, malicious code attached to a file, email or text sent over the Internet. When a recipient clicks on the link containing the malicious code, the worm is downloaded into the recipient's digital device, inflicting the permanent damage intended. This is among the most common terms in cybersecurity. Various types of Trojan horses have been explicitly created for a particular type of malicious activity.

Virtual Private Network (VPN). This is a paid subscribed service provided by many companies, allowing clients to connect to international servers/nodes distributed across the globe. Transmission and delivery of all types of data and voice communication are encrypted end-to-end.

Virus. A malicious code which replicates itself across the network system, inflicting the intended damage and fulfilling the objectives of the sender.

Vulnerability. Weakness in software codes. This could be a human error in writing code. Windows operating system, for example, has millions of lines of codes. Typically, 5-10% of vulnerabilities can be discovered and exploited by hackers. Reverse engineering is a method used by advanced programmers to identify such weaknesses.

White Hat Hackers. This term defines hackers who are working legally to examine computing systems and ensure that no vulnerabilities exist. They also assist in ensuring that systems are secure and not vulnerable to cyberattacks. They are also called ethical hackers.

WiFi. Software and hardware systems utilized by individuals, companies, governments and organizations to connect their digital devices, including computers, mobiles and any other types of digital devices using telecommunication systems provided by Internet service providers (ISPs). ISPs typically make it possible for such WiFi networks to be connected to the Internet. Public WiFi has become famously vulnerable to hackers, given its lack of security and identification of IP addresses of users within the public WiFi.

Worm. A malicious code sent across the Internet or an inside job. When delivered, it will inflict the required damage, depending on the intention of the code. It is similar to the virus in replicating itself and typically will have a payload that contains the malicious code.

Zero-Day. This term is used when a vulnerability is found in a software system or application. Hackers carry out reverse engineering on such software systems, find weaknesses and utilize them for hacking purposes. Weaknesses are discovered in various codes within applications, operating systems or multiple software systems implemented across an organization or used by individuals on their digital devices. It is estimated that there are at least 10% zero-day vulnerabilities in all applications or software systems. Many zero-day vulnerabilities have been discovered and fixed, and anti-viruses and firewalls updated.

Zombie. A term used for digital devices under the control of hackers. Such digital tools are used to launch attacks on targeted assets. The term is synonymous with Bots used in DoS/DDoS cyberattacks.

CHAPTER 2
Different Hacking Group Threats

Cyberattacks are attempted by many malicious actors. Regardless of the parties involved, one crucial consideration is reconnaissance efforts. Collecting enough information about the target asset, whether an individual or organization, is a mandatory stage in any successful cyberattack. This process involves the examination of computing infrastructures, either individual digital devices or the computing network system of an organization. Several tools of surveillance are available in the market to assist bad actors in this task. Hackers can thus obtain information and gain an insight into technical vulnerabilities, in order to choose the best methods to penetrate the victim's network system.

This chapter will explore the different threats represented by various groups of malicious actors. Hackers can be classified into three groups.

Amateurs. These are Green Hat Hackers. Interested actors who allocate enough time and effort to learning to hack can achieve a level of skill that can translate to specific threats. Green hat hackers can write codes which are not necessarily sophisticated, but they can achieve their mission. Most hacking attempts by mature actors may simply be malicious acts to test others' capabilities. Curiosity and the challenge to succeed, especially among young amateurs, are crucial factors encouraging them to become involved in hacking.

Amateurs are individuals or a group of good friends who find hacking attractive and are probably motivated by financial, social, economic and other interests. Their knowledge of the hacking process is acquired from taking online classes, studying printed materials and sharing their experience with friends in the dark web of hacker groups. There are also plenty of YouTube videos on the Internet which provide samples of hacking techniques for amateurs. All such publicly available learning information is valuable for hackers, enabling them to learn the craft.

Technically Skilled. The success of any cyberattack depends on the technical capability of the malicious actor (hacker). Amateur hackers can achieve similar results without having technical skills, as explained previously. However, failure rates are much higher. After acquiring enough technical information, technically skilled hackers can understand the different vulnerabilities of targets' assets. Being able to utilize various specialized hacking tools and techniques gives them higher success rates than those of amateur hackers.

These types of hackers acquire their technical skill and experience through working in specific organizations, such as intelligence gathering and cybersecurity contracting companies. They have formal education and/or extensive professional training in hacking. They have mastered hacking languages such as Kali and Python and may be an individual or a group.

Criminal Groups. Their mission is mostly financially motivated. Criminal groups may be involved in stealing credentials (user identification, passwords, PINs and other sensitive private information) to use in various illegal activities, including taking over bank accounts, ransoming, identity theft fraud and email phishing. Recruiting technically skilled hackers is part of their mission, enabling them to achieve their financial objectives. Phishing emails may be sent to a large number of acquired email addresses to scam people into sending them money, or a worm may be downloaded to access bank account information and other related financial data. They can also steal individual identities and use them illegally to issue forged documents. Due to the fact that the groups work underground, the hackers can operate from any country. These criminal entities may be state-sponsored. They pay the hackers large sums of money to carry out cyberattacks, while escaping legal responsibility if the hackers are caught. Many such groups have been identified by judicial authorities and declared wanted by legal authorities, but it is difficult to trace and bring them to justice.

Hacktivists. Their agenda is not financial but rather political and social. Believing they have justification for their activity enables them to work in harmony to achieve success in their mission, which is to expose the wrongdoing of nations, organisations and individuals to the public. Technical capability is one of the characteristics of this group and their activities are well planned. They are easily able to acquire and penetrate various types of networking systems. Anonymous and Wikileaks are two examples of this type of group. They work underground and it is not easy to locate and identify group members, although Wikileaks chairperson Julian Assange is well-known as the creator of the organization. Members of this group are also characterized by their ability to utilize more advanced cyberattack methods and tools. They have the important advantage of being able to operate from anywhere in the world and to use high encryption techniques in their communication and delivery of cyberattacks.

State-Sponsored. This group of hackers is the most effective and dangerous. They are classified as Advanced Persistent Threats (APT). There are two types: the first typically work within a unit or agency belonging to national intelligence services or the army. They are highly technically skilled people working in the field of cybersecurity. Due to unlimited resources, both financial and technological, these organizations can maintain well-qualified staff who have had advanced specialist training to sustain continuous cyberattacks. Nation state hacking groups will work on whatever agenda is required for them to enhance the country's program. This group is considered more offensive than defensive. Their mission can range from espionage to military actions. The most significant advantage of this group over all the others is that they have access to the technical means to reverse engineer all existing operating systems and software applications and identify all the zero-day vulnerabilities, as well as building an arsenal of viruses and worms. The group has the skills to write the necessary demons and unleash them. For example, if the mission is an espionage activity, then the code writers within the group will build an in-house code to be launched and remain in the network system in stealth status, which is hard for the targeted asset to discover. Advanced countries are in a much stronger position to take advantage of the capabilities of this group and utilize them effectively. Smaller and less developed countries are in the process of developing such groups and placing them in command and control cyber centers. However, due to the high costs involved, many of them will rely on third-party hacking groups to undertake their hacking missions, which serve the purposes of espionage, intelligence and military actions.

Individuals in third-party hacking groups are also classified as APT (Advanced Persistent Threats), since they are highly skilled hackers with persistent capabilities. They are for hire by different states and are paid large sums of money.

Black Hat Hackers. This group of hackers is considered extremely dangerous. Their mission is to hack into the computing environment, regardless of the legal consequences. They are technically skilled and have acquired the latest tools and techniques, enabling them to penetrate any secure networking system. Their success rate varies, depending on their technical skills. They operate in the shadows and work with the party that pays the most. Possessing a mission and agenda, they are likely to succeed if they are persistent. All groups which cause damage and have illegal access to established network systems are identified as black hat hackers.

White Hat Hackers. This group is also known as "ethical hackers". They are employed and hired by organizations to discover vulnerabilities in the computing environment. They know the methods and techniques used by the black hat group to hack into networking systems and launch malicious malworms. They employ technological tools and defense mechanisms to stop this illegal hacking or to minimize the damage that can be caused by viruses and worms. In penetration testing, organizations rely on white hat hackers to test the integrity and validity of the computing environment of an organization. The group will work with the legal authority mandated to them by the organization. Many cybersecurity firms and companies employ such groups to test the level of cybersecurity of the organization.

Gray Hat Hackers. This group can be black or white hat depending on the mission required by the entity which hires them. They also have APT technical skills. There needs to be a level of trust between the body hiring this group and its members, since the members can switch sides if there is no control or legal framework related to their mission.

CHAPTER 3
System Security Threats

There are various security threats to any computer or network system. As many as 90% of cyberattacks come from the online swamp of the Internet. The remaining attacks are not Internet related and rather computer crimes carried out directly within the local network system

Typically, attacks come from different sources. We must consider the ability of human beings with specific skills, either technical or in social engineering, which enable them to penetrate computing and networking systems quickly, overcoming technical resistance.

Human ability to penetrate computing and networking systems has been ahead of manufacturers' technical development capabilities. This is because of the difficulties in writing software codes that are perfect — most software systems are filled with holes and vulnerabilities due to code writing errors. Therefore, with reverse engineering and the ability of a highly technical person, it is always possible for bad actors to identify weaknesses and launch cyberattacks. There is no stopping Advanced Persistent Threats (APT) by hackers.

In ethical hacking, it is always the first job of the information technology manager to test the networking and computing environment to ensure that there are no remaining stealth viruses and worms in systems. Stealth viruses are the most dangerous as they are hard to discover.

Secondly, the manager must install proper security walls (firewalls) to stop or minimize any potential and future cyberattack, which is sure to happen sooner or later. Therefore, the information technology manager will actually penetrate the system as hackers do, to ensure a safe and clean computing system. Ethical hackers work for organizations to test system environments continuously and to ensure security.

Information technology managers and cybersecurity specialists must think like hackers if they want to provide security against cyberattacks. Behaving like a thief is how to catch a thief. Hackers usually look for vulnerabilities and weaknesses in the victim's computing system. The same thinking will enable the owners of systems to fill any gaps that exist.

There are several significant threats that can come from hackers, related to the following: human (i.e. social engineering), networks, hosts (servers), and applications/programs.

SOCIAL ENGINEERING

This is the process of using human intelligence to acquire information such as user identifications or passwords. Shoulder surfing is a good example, when a person stands behind another to find out his/her private information. It also includes guessing passwords, which may be done through having access to Facebook and social media, where information such as birth dates, pet names and names of loved ones is often used by thousands of people across the globe for their passwords.

To understand the concept of social engineering, we have defined the two words it constitutes. Social refers to the day-to-day lives of people, which include both the personal and professional. Engineering refers to the operation of performing a task by following specific steps and actions to achieve intended results.

Another way to describe social engineering is that it is a non-technical intrusion, relying heavily on human qualities to reveal sensitive and privileged information which compromises standard security procedures. Social engineering can be either human- or computer-based.

Human-based social engineering involves going to the targets and trying to get the maximum information possible about their credentials. People become vulnerable to these kinds of attacks when they carelessly leave behind personal data on social media. Computer-based social engineering is where hackers with technical skills utilize available tools to scan the victim's system and obtain the desired information.

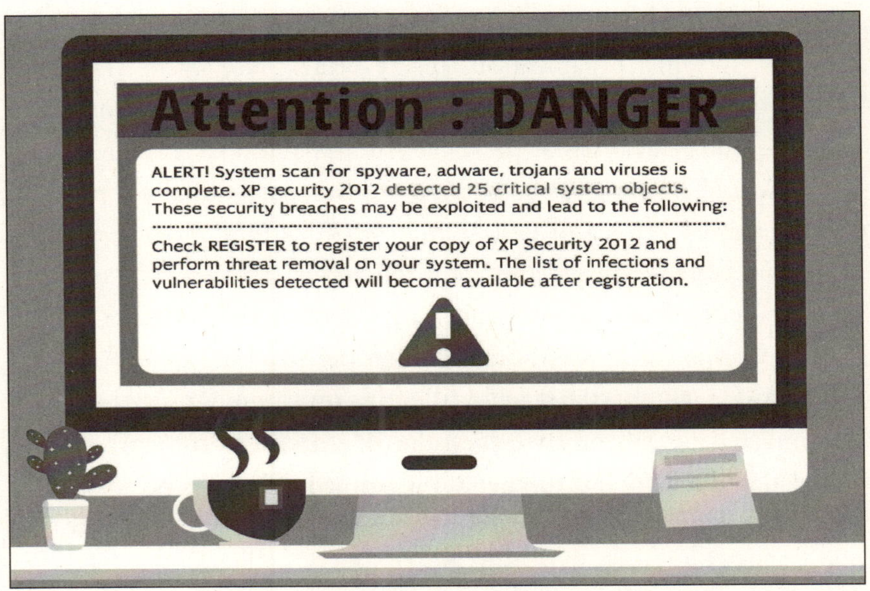

The above screen is a warning created by a hacker to trick victims or targeted entities into clicking on the hyperlink. If a victim clicks on it, then he or she will be directed to another web page explicitly created by hackers to collect credentials and personal information. By tricking the target victim into clicking on the link and leading them to a page cloned to look exactly like one from a website such as Facebook, the target victim will never know the difference between clone and real and will start to re-enter their user identification and password to access the Facebook page. All information entered is then stored in a file on the hacker's computer, ultimately to be used and manipulated. The question is, how has the hacker managed to do this? The tools existing in hacking languages allow them to do this. When clicking starts, not only is the victim redirected to a clone web page to enter their credentials, but also a worm is launched into their computer system.

INSIDE JOB ATTACKS

This type of cyberattack is typically performed within the target network system's organization. Inside attacks are orchestrated by employees who are not happy with their jobs and organizations. They have specific grievances or personal grudges and take revenge. Many sophisticated inside jobs are carried out by professional people who have mastered the art of penetrating organizations' sites physically. They are able to insert the required input devices into network systems. Individual inside jobs are easily detected and devices used to launch worms easily identified through the machine manufacturing code (MAC), which is the machine identification number. Furthermore, if connected to the Internet, then the IP (Internet Protocol) address can also be located and the person identified. The exceptions to this are when the inside job is performed on a device connected to the network that does not belong to the attacker.

PHISHING

This is the most common type of hacking. Hackers send phishing emails to hacked accounts with a link that contains a worm to be launched into the victim's computer system. Depending on the worm's payload, hackers' objectives are materialized when exploited. An example is to inform targeted victims that they have won a prize or a lottery, and when they click on a link to register their win or claim their prize, a worm is launched. The victim is then redirected to a web page in which they enter, for example, details of their bank accounts, names, addresses, banks and other personal information.

A Trojan horse is one of the most lethal worms. It is attached to an email, text message or any type of social media application and is launched when the victim opens an attached file or clicks on a link sent to them. Depending on its mission, it will search for particular library files containing vulnerabilities and exploit them. If its purpose is to spy on an intended victim, then it will look in specific libraries that are hidden (stealth). No anti-virus is able to find Trojan horse worms and clean the computer of them.

BACKDOOR

This type of worm is launched when a victim opens an attached file or a link containing the worm's payload. It enables a hacker to take control of the operating system and command line of the victim's computer, re-entering through this back door whenever he or she wishes. By taking control of the command line of the computer operating system in this way, the hacker can transfer, delete, change or shutdown the system; or spy on the victim, control the web camera or perform any other activities needed. Similarly, the backdoor is open when a hacker has managed to obtain a victim's personal credentials, mainly their passwords. However, if passwords are changed, the backdoor is closed.

WEBSITE CLONING

This is one of the most common techniques used by hackers to obtain credentials (user IDs and passwords). It involves cloning a website domain (name of an authorized website registered to a specific entity). This domain is registered legally and the name is exclusive to that particular body. However, given the advanced cloning tools available, a sophisticated hacker can copy the exact look and feel of a domain website and send a link to this website to an individual victim or large pool of victims, to farm their credentials. When the victim clicks on or opens a file containing specific messages, as shown in the chart earlier, the cloned website for the authorized entity will be displayed. The targeted victim will typically not know the difference between the real and the copied one. Since all websites require users to log in by entering their user identification, password and other security information, their private credentials will be accessed and stored by the hacker for later use.

WIFI HACKING

Wireless cyberattacks are becoming very popular with hackers, as the tools and techniques are readily available. The topic will be explored further in a chapter dedicated to the subject. The reason it is popular is because almost everyone using digital devices is connected daily on WiFi, whether at home or in offices, hospitals, airports, coffee shops or WiFi hotspots. Hacking into mobile devices such as laptops and mobile phones is a way of obtaining users' credentials and taking control of their devices.

DoS/DDoS

Both DoS (Denial of Service) and DDoS (Distributed Denial of Service) attacks have increased exponentially. They are commonly used by hackers to disable or deny service of a website or server that provides services to customers and clients. Simply put, DoS and DDoS attacks impact an individual server, making it shut down due to heavy traffic. In a DDoS attack, different machines which are connected to a command and control center are used to attack victims' sites, increasing the load of traffic sent, so that in a short time, the targeted server is frozen due to memory overload. These servers hijacked by hackers from different locations around the world are called zombies or slave computers. These machines have been taken over, using the simple hacking tools we described earlier. They are hijacked without their owners' knowledge and ordered to launch massive attacks, sending millions of requests to various targeted websites and servers, causing a freeze and denial of services. If these cyberattacks happen to servers used to connect an infrastructure, such as hospitals, schools, banks and transportation, the machines serving the infrastructure will not be able to perform. They will stop operating due to an overload. Computers have limited processing and memory powers. They cannot handle large requests coming to them within seconds and minutes. If zombie machines are used to attack banks' ATMs, telecommunication services and similar Internet-related services that we consider basic infrastructure services linked to daily activities of customers, this would be very inconvenient. If we then consider other types of services such as airlines, water, electricity and hospitals, then the damage to public services would be even more devastating. There are hundreds of government portals open to the public. If they were to shut down due to a DDoS attack, they would not be able to serve the public, causing certain panic, which is one of the desired goals of a country launching a cyberwar against another country. We have seen this happen in Estonia, Ukraine and in many countries around the world. In the past, countries suffering a DDoS attack have returned to operations in a couple of days or maybe hours. However, this has already changed; hackers have become more sophisticated. One method is to change the structure of worms and viruses with additional codes and instructions to launch more serious damage, not only to disable a server's operations but also to have them infect other connected computers, thus complicating the process of cleaning up and restoring attacked computers.

If they have hijacked victims' computers, hackers can also repeat such attacks. Then there are the state-sponsored hackers who have technical abilities to launch a worm with a DDoS attack and maintain a stealth presence as soon as they are inside targets' systems, thereby taking the hacking to the much higher level of cyber war. Only countries launching cyber wars can afford to acquire sophisticated cyber tools. Typically, state-sponsored cyberattacks will utilize a network of hackers. With the necessary finance behind them, they will be able to carry out cyberattacks from anywhere. No country which has launched a cyber war against another country has declared responsibility for it. The culprit always blames a rogue group of hackers who sympathize with it for making the attack.

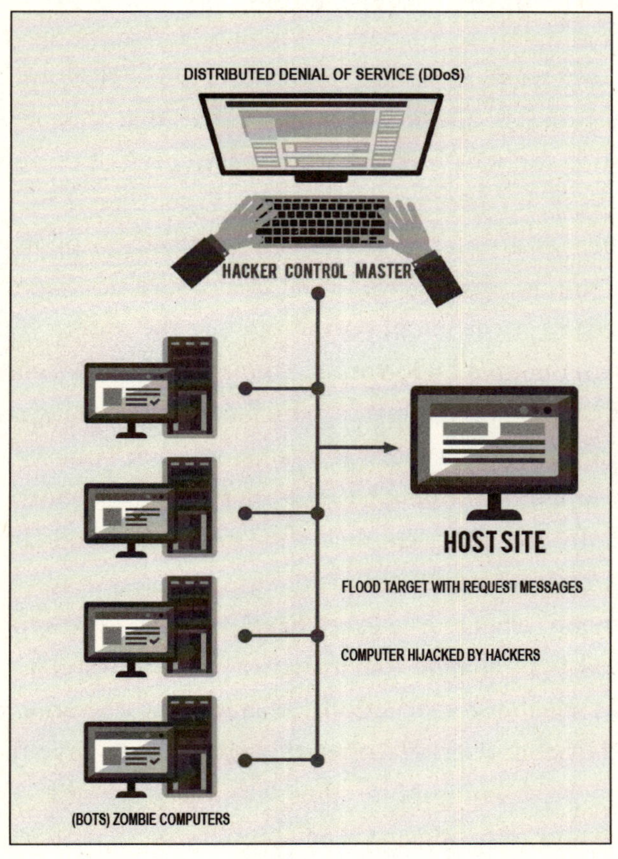

Escaping responsibility is easy for countries, due to the sophistication of the worms, viruses and hacking tools they employ. They will not leave behind evidence that will lead to them. Attacks come from zombie computers used by groups stationed in various other countries from the one launching the cyberwar. Even the Internet Protocol (IP) addresses displayed are international ones and do not belong to the attacking country.

SQL INJECTION/SCRIPTING

The latest and most effective of cyberattacks. SQL stands for Structured Query Language. By inserting a malicious written code into an existing website application or a database utilized by an organization, a malicious actor can then exploit the system, having gained illegal access. Hackers with technical skills can find vulnerabilities in a software system or application, including web-based ones, and inject a code to carry out certain activities such as file modification, transfer of records and manipulation of certain data, amongst other activities. For example, within banking and financial institutions, an injection of SQL can be effective in changing the currency of transaction from dollars into euros, for example, without the knowledge of the targeted institution. The discovery of such manipulation of currency units can have a devastating effect on the value of transactions undertaken. The transfer of records and files is done easily if a vulnerability is discovered in a database containing such records. Hackers can then use the records or files for future ransom activity.

RANSOMWARE

In recent years, this type of cyberattack has grown exponentially and caused huge damage to many industries and businesses around the world. WannaCry and PetaCry are examples of some of the attacks that have spread across the globe, resulting in substantial financial, economic and social turmoil. The concept of ransomware is to download a virus or worm into a victim's computer or digital device. It prevents the authorized owner of the equipment from accessing files and opening digital devices. A message appears on the device screen when the owner presses the start power button. The message typically states that the device is encrypted and inaccessible without a key. Specific instructions are displayed, advising the owner to transfer a certain amount, usually a few hundred dollars in digital currency, to a particular account using cryptocurrency. If the transaction is completed, then the device owner receives a key to unlock and decrypt the files and the device is restored to operation successfully. What has transpired here is that when the victim clicked on a link sent to them or opened an attached file, a ransom virus or worm was downloaded. A key then decrypts all records and documents. It stops the owner of the device from accessing them unless payment instructions are followed successfully, and the decrypted key is sent to the victim to enter and get the equipment back in its original form.

CHAPTER 4
Password Security

This topic is the most important when it comes to cybersecurity and has the least attention paid to it. Although technical-minded people are very aware of the importance of choosing a password that has a combination of characters (alphanumerics) made up of symbols, letters and numbers, many users, either individually or within organizations, unfortunately resort to simple passwords that they can remember and type conveniently into their digital devices. Given the fact that we have so many applications, software systems and digital devices, we choose passwords familiar to us, such as birth dates, pet names, the city we were born in, names of father, mother, children or any other familiar people that the brain can easily recall, so that we do not need to resort to passwords written down and stored somewhere we cannot locate. Many of us do not remember passwords and unfortunately go back to the account manager of the application or software system in order to obtain them. Many of us do not change our password frequently, due to lack of understanding, although this is highly recommended.

It has become very easy for hackers and individuals using social engineering to obtain passwords. With social media and various apps that are utilized and the fact that each one of them requires a password, users of social media apps have their life spread all over the Internet. Information about users' lives is available on the World Wide Web and it is simple for beginner hackers to use this publicly available information to assemble the password through trial and error. Many smart social engineering hackers can easily figure out the password by collecting enough information belonging to the targeted person.

Furthermore, there are a number of tools and hacking techniques available to smart hackers to enable them to access the passwords of individuals, regardless of their complexity.

Passwords are considered the holy grail of credentials that criminal hackers would like to acquire. When this objective is achieved, the account or access to it is under the control of the hackers. They can choose not to prevent the original owner of the account from accessing it and can choose to access it themselves anytime they want; or they may take over the account entirely, and in this case the authorized owner is out of luck and will not be able to get back into it. In this case, the only option is to contact the application owner/developer to report the hacking incident and lack of access, which is a very difficult task to achieve, with lengthy procedures, but possible. Hopefully, the owner of the account who is locked out has a backup for the lost files and documents, which can be restored and placed into a new account.

TWO-FACTOR AUTHENTICATION

Many organizations resort to additional security passwords to enhance the level of security. For example, in addition to a user identification (ID) and a password, there will be additional information needed for secure access, such as a pin number, thumb print, voice, a facial picture and other keys. If a hacker discovers the right password for a victim, then he/she must acquire the additional password key to successfully access the account. This will make a cyberattack more difficult. Unfortunately, a large number of users do not resort to a third level (three-factor authentication), due to the difficulties of remembering multiple passwords and security keys.

Many individual users who have several accounts, especially for social media applications, will only have a password for each account, typically similar in nature, and this makes hacking easy. However, companies and government entities have resorted to three-factor authentication to ensure a higher level of password security. It is noticeable that small organizations do not add additional authentication factors and are therefore susceptible to hacking.

Many companies have accepted the notion that the current user identification login (ID) and password are not enough to secure digital devices and they have added another code or PIN number that is required to access the device. If hackers manage to acquire the ID and password, it will be more difficult for them to access the account without having the PIN code which is usually sent to a mobile number or user account. However, even that is not hard for technically advanced hackers who have already managed to hack into the user's accounts and probably their mobile phones too.

PASSWORD CHANGING

Given the increased frequency of password attacks, awareness has grown in recent years of the need to change passwords often. This can take place voluntarily or be forced by the system within an organization every three months. For example, a message will be displayed on the screen of an authorized user within a network system in an organization, instructing users to change their passwords within a certain time frame, and if this does not happen, the user will be locked out of the system and will have to call the network administrator to reactivate access to the account with a temporary password, and then enter a new personal password.

Many users will click on the option of having the digital device update and store the password in its memory, since they do not want to bother with entering the password every time they access an account.

Such a feature is a gift for hackers. Whenever a computer or digital device (mobile) is controlled by hackers, this feature of memory recall of passwords for all accounts on such devices is then under their control.

It is therefore highly recommended to change passwords more frequently to eliminate the risk of cyberattacks.

BAD PASSWORD HABITS

As stated earlier, a bad password habit is when a user resorts to a familiar password that is easy to remember, and examples of these have already been given. A list of the most common passwords has been published on the Internet, and commonly used passwords such as the ones listed below are easily guessed by hackers.

MOST COMMON YAHOO PASSWORDS

Word frequency, sorted by count, top 10

Word	Count	Of total
123456	1667	0.3764 %
password	780	0.1761 %
welcome	437	0.0987 %
ninja	333	0.0752 %
abc123	250	0.0565 %
123456789	222	0.0501 %
12345678	208	0.047 %
sunshine	205	0.0463 %
princess	202	0.0456 %
qwerty	172	0.0388 %

PASSWORD LENGTH AND COMPLEXITY

When authorized users of accounts utilize such common passwords, they make themselves vulnerable to cyberattacks and therefore the length and complexity of password selection becomes essential. Depending on the ability of users to remember such passwords without relying on the digital device to recall passwords saved in its memory becomes a daunting challenge. This explains why simple passwords are used by millions of Internet users. The lengthier passwords are, containing a complex combination of words, numbers and symbols, the harder it is for hackers to simply guess them through trial and error. Also, working out such passwords using social engineering, based on individual social media accounts, will not be easy.

ENCRYPTED PASSWORDS

A password is considered good if it will require the same amount of work as a 64-bit encryption key. This is made up of 64 characters, which is long for users to enter into their systems, for example into their email accounts. Hackers will have difficulty if a password is encrypted with a key and changed from being eight to 64 characters. We can say in this case that the password is secure. However, there is always the chance that such encrypted passwords can and will be decrypted and reversed by various tools and techniques to figure out its original characters.

BRUTE FORCE

This technique of forcing and breaking a complex and encrypted password and reversing it to its original state is well practiced by hackers. Technical knowledge is required to use such techniques. Legal authorities have used brute force tools to break encrypted and unknown security keys and passwords to get into digital devices, either computers or mobile devices.

Applying brute force means that high processing power, like that of a super computer, is used to crack complex combinations of characters. However, most users, as mentioned, do not resort to such complex passwords. They usually have passwords of between eight to 18 characters. Organizations also ask their staff to use a low number of characters to make passwords easier to remember.

HASHING

Hashing is used to transform a string of characters into a usually shorter fixed-length value or key that represents the original string.

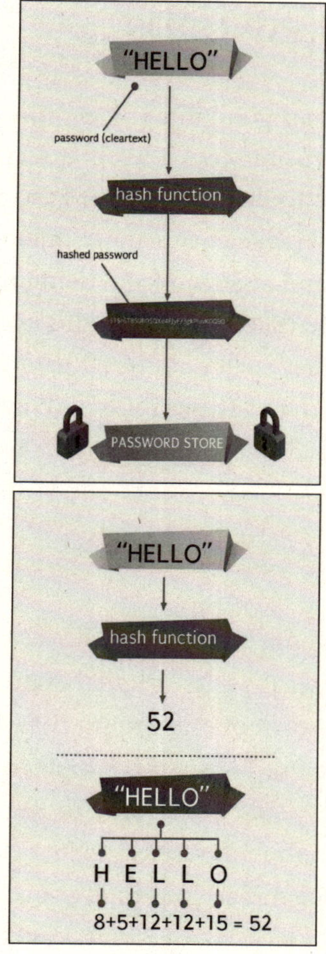

This hashing technique has become standard for many organizations which value the importance of password protection. Every organization has a number of users and they all have either one or multiple passwords. When keeping a record of such collective passwords in a database, it is important that the passwords are not stored in a readable form, such as plain text. They must be in an unreadable form for anyone within the organization or outside it. Therefore, the hashing technique as described above is applied. This transforms all passwords into unreadable form. If and when a hacker gains access to a password table, it will be difficult to figure out which user has which password. In order to transform this unreadable form into plain readable text, brute force as described above is needed.

Password protection is an urgent and important function for any computer networking system. Awareness and education about how properly to manage and update passwords of individuals and organizations have become top of the list activities, in order to maximize cybersecurity.

CONCLUSION

Recent reports estimate that 52 percent of digital device users will enter the same familiar passwords which are easy to remember, or ones with only small modifications to the original passwords, in most of their devices. This trend of having similar passwords is what makes life easier for hackers. Furthermore, the reports also mention that there are over 5.2 million accounts on the Internet. Online accounts of major consumer stores, credit card companies, email providers, and many other sources have been hacked. These online user account credentials are either for sale on the dark web or traded amongst hackers. Criminal groups also use them for phishing and other criminal activities such as identification fraud.

Certain measures can be taken in order to make online credentials more secure when using digital devices. They include:

1. Updating your digital devices with the latest software, ensuring that certain discovered vulnerabilities are patched.
2. Changing the manufacturers' passwords which come with many digital devices to your own.
3. Ensuring that your passwords are different and long enough. Keeping a paper or digitally stored file for them.
4. Frequently changing passwords. It is recommended that they are changed every three months.
5. Using a password manager software system. If you are dealing with many digital devices, this system will enable the software to select a password for you randomly and remember it for each device.
6. Using two-factor authentication login. This will help make hacking harder, although it is not impossible to break.
7. When you select a new password, the operating system will give you the option of saving this new password in memory as a cookie, and every time you log into your application, the password is recalled, however it is not recommended.

CHAPTER 5
Viruses and Malware

Viruses and malware are common terms in today's cybersecurity. They are used interchangeably, but there are some specific technical differences between them.

A virus is a malicious code written by a hacker with the mission of replicating itself. When launched into a computer network system, it attaches itself to a program or the files of an operating system. A malware or worm is a malicious code similar to a virus. The difference is that it has a payload that is attached to a file, document or text. When these are opened or a link is clicked, the payload containing the malicious code is downloaded and activated.

Malware contains many viruses and worms. Therefore, it has become difficult to distinguish between the two terms.

Examples of malware include Trojan horse, backdoor, spyware, ransomware, botnet, crypter and adware. Some of these terms have been defined in Chapter One.

MALICIOUS CODES

Historically, malicious codes (viruses or worms) started when the computer was invented. Amateur individuals took on the challenge of writing malicious codes in the computer language coding system to see if it was possible to enter into the system and disrupt or damage it. There was no Internet 20 years ago and "crackers" (the terms used at the time) did not have online access into a computer system. The only way to launch the malicious codes was to physically access a workstation wired into the main computer system. The codes were simple and did not do much damage, except that they could look at documents and download them.

The writing of malicious codes (viruses and worms) became more sophisticated in the context of the army and intelligence agencies, who wanted to weaponize them in times of war. Also, with widespread Internet usage and increasing numbers of applications, hackers as they are now called started to acquire the technical skills necessary to write much more sophisticated malicious codes. The damage caused by such codes is well documented and they have become even more dangerous in times of war and conflicts between nations.

ZERO-DAY VULNERABILITIES

The term zero-day does not relate to the number zero or any particular day. Rather, it indicates that there is a weakness or hole in the software and hardware systems used by companies and organizations.

Zero-day vulnerabilities typically exist in any software and hardware system, but we can say that most such weaknesses exist in software systems. Most software programs are written in multiple codes (hundreds and millions). Typically, if there is a one million code written for a software program (operating system, database, application, a utilities and maintenance program) there is the possibility that 5-10% vulnerabilities exist. This is due to the fact that human beings writing such codes make certain errors which are considered weaknesses. This is where the skills of advanced hackers and the reverse engineering of such programming codes reveal holes, enabling hackers to take advantage and launch viruses and worms. These holes are called zero-day vulnerabilities.

ZERO-DAY ATTACKS

Hackers and nation states rely heavily on zero-day vulnerabilities to find a way to enter systems, launch virus and worm payloads, maintain existence within systems and clear their traces at the end if necessary.

Most past, present and future cyberattacks and hacking are the results of zero-day exploits. Hackers look at a new software system and examine the code lines to determine if there is a vulnerability to exploit. In 2016, a hacking group called the Shadow Brokers claimed to have obtained the NSA's best hacking tools and offered them on the dark web and social media. The same tools used by state-sponsored groups and intelligence and law enforcement agencies for spying upon their citizens, both individuals and groups, at home and abroad, were stolen and offered to the highest bidder. Some of these zero-day vulnerabilities were shared with other hackers, such as the famous WannaCry ransomware virus (2017). It is important to realize that these zero-day exploits are not easy. Hackers must acquire the source code of the software system when it is launched. At that point, software engineers and forensic analysts determine if the original writers of the software program have forgotten something or if there is a missing link or hole through which a hacker can get in and attach a virus payload to files, thereby taking control of the victim's system. The source of any program or application is considered a trademark property of the developer and it has a copyright, which is protected by law. However, in the United States, as well as in almost every country in the world, obtaining the source code for national security and spying purposes is done either through specific licensing agreements with the software developer or by hacking into the company that developed the software system and downloading it. Either way, obtaining the source code of a software system is the first step, and then software engineers and hacking specialists can exploit zero-day vulnerability.

We have seen famous zero-day exploits in the Windows operating system, where the Stuxnet worm was used to exploit four Windows vulnerabilities. The countries which planned and executed the attack on the Iranian nuclear facility managed to disable over 60 percent of its ability to enrich nuclear uranium. Another famous exploit compromised Adobe Flash Player along with Internet Explorer, Chrome, Firefox and Safari. One of the easiest ways to find zero-day vulnerability is to hack into the companies and organizations which have obtained and stored them in their databases. For example, recently a hacker using the online name "Phineas Fisher" managed to hack into Gamma International, a company well-known for offering advanced spyware to governments. The hacking team managed to steal tens of gigabytes of data, including the infamous "FinFisher" surveillance software, used by many developed and developing countries globally.

PEGASUS TECHNICAL CAPABILITIES

Pegasus technical capabilities supersede any surveillance hacking tool. Below is a list of its technical capabilities, which have also been listed in a 40-page document (manual) which was leaked and published on the Internet.

Given its startling capabilities, it is unsurprising that many governments are eager to acquire it.

Pegasus can do the following:

1. Extract data and information (without the mobile phone owner's knowledge) and without any trace back to the hackers.
2. Ability to self-destruct when there is a hint of detection.
3. View all activities of the phone.
4. Download all types of data, including text, photo, video and any materials on the phone.
5. Organize the data in a calendar style review and create alerts in tracked activities.

6. Keep a log of all calls which are listened to online or recorded.
7. Provide a dashboard to track location activities and movements by controlling the GPS on the phone.
8. Provide a map showing all tracked movements and activities.
9. Monitor when the owner types or pushes any of the buttons on the phone.
10. Enable viewing and monitoring of the hacked phone in real time.

All this takes place without the owner of the mobile phone feeling or detecting any change in the phone's behavior. The Israeli Defense Department uses Pegasus in most of its activities. It has deployed it in the various branches of its military, including the air force, navy and army, as well as, of course, all internal and Mossad security services. Israel created a very secretive unit named 8-200, which is responsible for cybersecurity.

IDENTITY INTRUSION (THEFT AND FRAUD)

Mobile phones have become part of our daily activities. Many people spend long hours on their phone following social media, as mentioned. Being connected to friends, family and the world has become imperative to our daily life. A great deal of information, much of it very private and sensitive, such as family photos, videos, bank information and other information determining your identity, such as passport and identification card information, can be extracted from phones and used in criminal and espionage activities.

When your identity is violated and your personal information gathered illegally or for national security reasons which are considered legal by the government, your identity and all your stored data, as well as all your activities, are out in the open for hackers to see. Phone data can potentially be manipulated to achieve an agenda that can impact levels of national security. For example, if the target (victim) is an individual in an important government or military position and altered messages or emails are sent from their phone without their knowledge, then the risks are high. Just imagine.

GROWTH OF CYBER WARFARE

Cyber warfare has become important to national security in many countries around the world. More than 45 countries have bought Pegasus spyware from the Israeli surveillance company NSO. A number of companies similar to NSO have also sold their spying tools to different countries. After the secret of the source code of Pegasus was discovered by Citizen Lab in Canada, the spying capabilities of these powerful tools was revealed.

THE WANNACRY VIRUS

The WannaCry worm is a ransomware worm that works in the phishing style of hacking. A computer user receives an email with a link which, when clicked, immediately launches a payload containing the virus. The objective is to disable the computer after decrypting all files and documents. Victims then receive a screen message with instructions for them to pay a ransom using the digital currency Bitcoin, sending it to a particular location. If the victim fails to follow the instructions and cooperate within a specified time frame, a second message will be displayed in which the ransom is doubled, and this is the last warning that without payment the victim's computer will be completely inoperable and all documents and files lost. If the machine owner follows the instruction and pays, then he or she receives a key enabling the machine to operate normally again and all files and documents are decrypted.

DIGITAL SPYING TOOL: PEGASUS

As mentioned above, the Israeli company, NSO, developed this powerful spying tool, designed to be used against local and foreign residents. It has also been used for surveillance of high target individuals. The Israeli government has classified Pegasus as a weapon.

The Pegasus manual states that it is able to monitor virtually any popular app, including but not limited to: Facebook, Twitter, Pinterest, Google+ and Instagram.

Pegasus specializes in hacking into mobile devices. It is very expensive to use, given the highly technical nature of the worm and the large number of mobile devices it can track.

The most well-known social media application it is used for is WhatsApp, as this is used by over a billion and a half people, but it is not exclusive to this app, and as stated previously it can be employed for all applications.

The software system used for constructing this spying tool is a sophisticated coding system.

Citizen Lab is an interdisciplinary laboratory based in Canada which works on tracking Internet threats against civil society. Citizen Lab acquired the Pegasus codes from the phone of a Saudi citizen residing in Canada. His phone was hacked by Saudi Arabia, one of the countries which had acquired Pegasus. In reverse engineering of the Pegasus coding system, it was found that Pegasus exploits the kernel, hides itself in the root and exploits vulnerabilities in various mobile applications. When examined using Jail Break technique (Jailbreak), it was discovered that Pegasus takes over the phone security mechanism and hides itself (Stealth) by controlling the operating system, memory stack and heap of the phone.

When NSO was asked why they had sold this spying weapon to so many countries, they claimed that it is designed to be used for crime and terrorism prevention and any misuse is prohibited.

However, the fact remains that governments have used Pegasus to serve national security agendas internally and internationally without any recourse to and in violation of any such agreement with NSO.

ANTI-VIRUSES AND FIREWALLS

When a virus or worm (malicious code) is written and launched, it must have certain objectives in the mind of the hacker launching it. These objectives may be financial gain, vandalism, cyber terrorism, fulfilling a political agenda and others.

There are a number of anti-viruses employed in computer systems and digital devices which are able to stop or minimize the threats and potential damage inflicted by these malicious codes. Most anti-viruses sold by cybersecurity companies perform similar tasks in filtering all communication in and out of the network system and into the Internet. The worry of course is that a large number of data communications coming from the World Wide Web (the Internet) can and will contain malicious codes, and it is the job of such anti-viruses to stop them. The anti-virus systems have modules and scanners that look up the digital signatures of such malicious codes to see if they match ones stored in tables of malicious code digital signatures. If they match, then the data communication will not enter the network system and will instead be diverted into other stored files to be logged for analysis. For example, a typical anti-virus would have anti-spyware, anti-Trojan, anti-phishing, email scanners and sensors. They are effective in detecting such malicious codes and digital signatures. These anti-virus software programs are highly recommended in any network system or digital device as a protection against cyberattacks.

FIREWALLS

These are must-have hardware and software systems in any organization. They complement the existing anti-virus but are not to be used in individual laptops or digital devices. They are mainly employed in an organizational context (by companies or government entities) with multiple users in a network system. They are more powerful than anti-viruses as they represent a wall stopping all types of malware from entering the system. They excel in minimizing cyberattack threats. They do not come cheap, and the more organizations invest in them, the more cybersecurity they can maintain. Although not bulletproof solutions, they are nevertheless effective.

COUNTER MEASURES

The above anti-viruses and firewalls are considered part of the counter measures implemented by any organization or individual utilizing digital devices and connected to the Internet. There are additional tools and software systems such as Intrusion and Detection Systems (IDS) that can be purchased and employed to strengthen cybersecurity, but they are expensive.

Furthermore, policies and procedures alongside user awareness programs and education must be deployed to inform users not to open suspicious email and file attachments, or on social media, not to click on any link attached to a text message or download a video or graphic attachment that might contain a malicious code through which viruses and worms are downloaded and activated.

CHAPTER 6
Email Security

The email system that we use either on our computer workstations, laptops or mobile devices is one of the most effective means of communication individually and organizationally. The need to communicate between individuals using email started prior to the launch of the Internet. When the US army (Pentagon) wanted to communicate with military posts and send them messages and files, there was a need to establish a secure email system and this was achieved through the (ARPNET) Advanced Research Project in the 1960s. Furthermore, academia started noticing the need to communicate for the purpose of research and development, and to exchange messages, files and documents. Communication was simple and limited in capabilities. However, now with the advancement of the Internet and the capability of Internet service providers (ISP) to provide fast and effective communication links, the email system has become indispensable not only socially, but also economically.

SECURITY LEVEL

When the email system is offered by software developers as part of the standard package when one purchases a computer unit, or when an organization introduces a company-wide email system, the intention is that security is provided, given that a sender of an email will have a direct one-to-one link with the receiver, or a one-to-many type of link. Such lines of communication of a local area network using cables were supposed to be highly secure and there was no need for any concern about the integrity and validity of the data transmitted. This changed when communication using email began over the Internet.

The Internet has meant that almost all users of the email system now understand that communication using it might not be secure. Internet applications such as Yahoo, Gmail and Hotmail which provide email accounts will not guarantee the delivery and accuracy of any email sent or received. Millions of user email accounts have been compromised, copied, sold and hacked by third parties. The level of email security as we once knew it has changed.

If anyone asks you if your email system is secure, the answer is definitely not at all. Why is this? Some of the answers are below.

PHISHING

This technique of hacking into an account started early on when a group of criminals started sending emails to people across the world after acquiring their account addresses. These emails were known as the “Nigerian Letter”. This letter says that there is a chance for the recipient to make lots of money if he or she can help with a transfer of money from certain countries from which the money could not be released for certain reasons. The incentive for going along with this scam is that 10% of the money, if successfully transferred, will be yours. The trick is that you will be asked to provide certain banking information and a transfer of a small amount as an administrative fee for the transfer. Many people have fallen for such scams, unaware that now not only can their banking information be copied into fake checks and used internationally, but also the funds transferred will not be returned.

Another more advanced example of phishing is widespread globally. It originates from criminal groups which hack into email accounts and understand how the victim writes and communicates. Most email systems contain the contact addresses of friends, relatives and business associates. An email will be sent to the victims from the hacked contact list, written as if it came from the real sender and claiming that they are in a critical situation and require financial assistance, since they are abroad and have lost all their belongings or been robbed. The email requires the victim to send money to a specific bank account. This type of phishing scam has been very successful. Most such scams are sent out internationally with fake Internet addresses (IP) and it is therefore hard for legal authorities to trace the culprit.

Yet another example is the email letter sent by a CEO of a bank to a financial controller with certain instructions and documentation to transfer money to a certain account. The email is not actually from the CEO but from a criminal hacker who has accessed the email account of the CEO and copied his/her style of writing. The financial controller is not aware of the scam and believes that the email has come from the CEO. Unfortunately, trusting the email system and not picking up the phone and calling the sender to confirm if the order for the transfer has come from an authorized sender has caused a great deal of financial and social damage.

THE BULGARIAN HACK

The country of Bulgaria has a population of seven million people. In 2019, the National Revenue Service, a government database containing registration details of over five million citizens, was hacked and all the information became available on the World Wide Web.

This hack was a major embarrassment to the government of Bulgaria because sensitive information such as birth dates, residency, the full profile of every citizen and other vital personal information had been compromised and become available to everyone to see and use. The government is currently investigating what happened. One suspected individual has been arrested and interrogated. However, the damage has been done and it is catastrophic. Many government officials will be sacked because of this huge data breach. The email addresses of five million citizens of Bulgaria are now available for criminal groups to utilize for phishing activities. One solution to this problem would be for those affected to immediately change their email addresses, in the hope that phishing has not already happened.

This proves that email security is critical for keeping digital devices safe from hacking. When a hacker obtains your email address, there is a greater chance that you will receive an email which seems to be from someone you know well, and you may not doubt the identity of the sender. When you open an attached file or a link provided, a virus and loaded worm will be downloaded into your system. Your digital device then becomes the property of the hacker.

EMAIL ENCRYPTION

Most of our email systems, such as Yahoo, Gmail and Hotmail, do not provide the latest encryption protection algorithm. Some of them indicate that end-to-end encryption is available and can be obtained by a subscription fee. If you use an email account which is free, you will not get encryption and protection. Many organizations have email systems that are easy to decipher. Typically, in current software systems designed for many enterprises, email accounts have become standardized. For example, the use of first name and last name separated by a dot is common. Thus, it is easy for hackers to download the list of employees of an enterprise and figure out their email addresses. Some organizations allow employees to choose their email address names which are also not difficult to guess, as many staff use their first and last names in a combination of letters. By trial and error, hackers can work out the full email addresses.

There are encryption systems that can be added to email systems.

The encryption algorithms will allow email communication to be encrypted from senders to receivers. This will make it hard for hackers to send email, even if they acquire the email address for an account. They will have to figure out the style of writing and add the required file or link containing the malicious codes. It is therefore advisable to install such encryption systems in enterprises. But for individuals, we still have to face the fact that our email communications are not really encrypted and are open to attacks by hackers.

EMAIL ANTI-VIRUSES

Every email system should have this feature. There are many anti-viruses that can protect the digital devices of individuals from spam and other unwanted email sent over the Internet. These anti-viruses scan the emails coming via the Internet and reject or redirect suspicious emails to a junk folder. Ordinary email users may notice that many emails from websites specializing in pornography, drugs, food, medicine and gambling, and other suspicious websites and unknown sources do not arrive in your inbox, but are deposited in a junk folder. This is because these emails are scanned by the anti-virus. It scans the heading, including the sender, receiver and subject, and directs suspicious emails to junk folders, but when emails are sent from familiar sources that are considered authentic and have normal headings, they will be allowed into your inbox.

Organizations which invest in cybersecurity employ the latest email anti-virus software systems. If an email gets through a firewall, the anti-virus can pick it up and redirect it to a junk folder. Again, similar to the individual email system, when phishing is used by hackers, it means that the email account has already been compromised and hackers will try and send an email representing an authentic sender, hoping that the receiver (victim) will immediately open it, thus enabling the downloading of a virus or loaded worm into the system.

SIMPLE PROTECTION

The recommendation for an average email user is never to trust an email sent by anyone asking the user to transfer funds or perform a particular activity outside their normal practice. It is advisable not to open the document attached to the email or to click a link within the email without calling the sender and confirming that the email is coming from the right party. Many people do not bother to do this, which is a mistake. They tend either to ignore the email, which could be legitimate, or proceed with opening it, putting themselves at risk of hacking.

For organizations, the email system has better protection, since organizations invest in email scanning tools and anti-viruses, as well as firewalls. However, they are also vulnerable to phishing, since email addresses are easy to figure out, as explained earlier. Phishing can take place because staff email addresses can become available to hackers. For example, a finance manager could receive a request from a manager higher up in the chain of command to transfer funds. The finance manager typically will not question the authenticity of the email received, and the rest is history if he decides to open the email and look at the attachment or press the link included in the email, which has been sent by a hacker.

There is no way to make an email system completely safe. Many issues which occur are due to human weaknesses, and therefore awareness and education are keys for ensuring better protection against criminal hackers who exploit the email security system.

CHAPTER 7

Internet Security

Internet security relates to all activities carried out over the Internet. This can include your browser activities in searching websites or accessing information using a search engine. It also includes the use of Internet Protocol (IP) security and various digital devices with machine addresses (MAC) codes that identify the device/s where the communication starts and ends. There are many Internet security issues, not only hardware device-related but also related to software and application systems.

INTERNET SECURITY BREACHES

Whenever you are online on the Internet, and this is happening 24/7 on any one of the digital devices which are available, such as laptops or mobile devices, you are constantly connected to one type of application or browser. This means that with or without your knowledge, you will be receiving and sending streams of data, even if this is just a confirmation that you are online.

Let us take an example. If you purchase a laptop or mobile device, as part of the setup you have connection to Internet, either using WiFi or an email account set up system. Also, you will be activating many types of social media applications in order to share and communicate with friends and other connected users.

Another example is when you go online shopping or order an Uber taxi or food delivery. Here also you are connected to the

Internet. Our life as we know it would not be as functional and smooth without the Internet.

The Internet of Things (IOT) has added more complexity to our life in terms of devices that used to be offline and mechanical. Now they have digital chips and wireless communications connected to your router. You can turn on your refrigerator, microwave and TV, for example, using digital devices such as mobile phones. They are connected using WiFi and Bluetooth. There are central servers which provide continuous connectivity so that users do not have to constantly set up.

GOOD AND BAD

We believe that technology will make our life easier and is a good thing to have. We live in a comfortable state where all types of applications are at our fingertips. Since we are constantly on the move, our mobile digital devices are attached to us and we are always connected to the Internet as we move around. We always check to see if our digital devices are on and connected. If we do not have an Internet connection on our mobile phone, for example, then we will search for places where there are WiFi capabilities. We also now have the ability to create our own hotspots using the Internet service provider when we cannot connect to existing WiFi due to password protection limitation.

This means that wherever you are, you will find a way to be connected, either at home or outside. In the old days, when traveling on a plane, people could not utilize their digital devices. Calling or sending text messages were limited to airline communication devices installed on the seats of the aircraft. Airplanes now have Internet data communication, utilizing satellite technology, not only to facilitate more advanced fixed communication on the flight, but also enabling travelers to use personal digital devices such as mobiles and laptops. Connection to the Internet is now available 24/7.

Now, the bad part of using such wonderful technology is the danger of having your digital devices compromised and hacked when you are online. Over 90% of hacking and data breaches are generated from the Internet. It is estimated that the annual cost of cybercrime exceeds 1 trillion US dollars.

Imagine that in your house, which is a smart home, all digitally controlled devices such as electronic doors, refrigerators, oven, TVs, microwave, and even your alarm system are compromised, because of a cyberattack on the server/node that is controlling them. This means that the hacker who compromised them now has control over these devices, just as the authorized owner had. Later in this book, we will give more details about how hackers are able to do this, but essentially they have managed to obtain access to credentials such as passwords and other security aspects of Internet connectivity.

Invasion of privacy and fraud are highly likely whenever your credentials are compromised and hacked by criminal groups and technically advanced individuals.

THE CASE OF THE PUERTO RICO GOVERNOR

In 2019, the mobile phone of Governor Ricardo Rosselló of Puerto Rico was hacked. All communications from the Governor in and out using the social media application Telegram were made publicly available. This revealed 900 pages of chat containing homophobic expressions and attacks on political rivals.

The public in Puerto Rico took to the street and demonstrated, demanding his resignation. The Governor apologized and was later forced to resign. However, due to the fact that he did not deny the existence of such messages, it means they were genuine, and hackers had a political agenda to make them public and bring down the Governor and his government.

In this case, technically skilled hackers were able to expose corrupt government officials, which many people might consider a good thing. However, it is also possible for Internet capabilities to be used against us, as in cases of fraud and identity theft. An even more serious issue arises when not only is a person's identity used criminally, but it can be traded and sold across the Internet, causing significant economic and social damage.

BROWSER SECURITY

Users access the Internet using one of the many browsers available on laptops and mobile devices. Examples are the popular Google Chrome, Mozilla Firefox, Opera, Safari and Microsoft Internet Explorer.

Many users unfamiliar with browser security take usage and accessibility offered by these browsers for granted and are unaware of the dangers of using them. Security breaches and hacking can occur when, for example, a user clicks on a browser to search for a topic or reach a particular website.

HTTP VS HTTPS

Many users unaware of Internet browser security do not pay attention to the http line when they enter a website or a reference search. If you see that the http:// line does not have the letter (s) at the end, https, it means that what you are looking at or searching for is not secured. When you see https:// before your website or reference search, then the access is secured.

The security issue of http protocol means that any hackers who would like to read the packet of data sent and received by the http protocol can and will be able to read it in plain text, i.e., in plain English or any other language. When there is https, then the packet of data is encrypted by an algorithm and must be decrypted and converted into plain text in order to read it.

INTERNET SECURITY DILEMMA

There is a battle between those who want to provide maximum security for Internet users and those criminal individuals and groups who use the Internet as a playground in which to carry out all kinds of criminal activities. On the one hand, authorities and Internet application providers try to ensure that all data packets transmitted and received via the Internet have some level of security, but on the other, hackers and other actors try to take advantage of loopholes in Internet structures and applications used publicly across the World Wide Web.

Many organizations struggle with the concept of offering Internet access to their workers. Although they value the Internet as a means of communication and a source of valuable information, there is always the fear that making such technical means available to connected users will result in actions by bad actors that might compromise the computing system and ultimately impact the organization financially and operationally. The balance between having Internet access and, at the same time, security in the organization's computing network systems is very difficult to achieve and requires constant investment and oversight by highly technically skilled people working within the organization's computing environment.

Both individuals and countries are affected by this scenario. In the case of individuals, there is no escape from using the Internet, especially with the widespread usage of social media applications. From a young age, individuals are hooked up to their mobile devices, and there is a trend in this direction even with those over 50. Mobile devices have become an integral part of communications, and one notices that people are constantly using their digital devices, intentionally or unintentionally. Social media pushes mobile users to interact, and thus demand is constantly increasing for more such interaction, and more powerful devices are needed to accommodate the huge number of data packets transmitted and received over the Internet.

There is a dilemma for organizations with users who are connected to local area networks and use their mobile devices to access various organizations' websites and applications. Dependency on mobile devices such as laptops and mobile phones is increasing. International companies have various offices and employees of such companies travel across the globe, requiring Internet connection in order to access each other and the various servers/nodes of the company's network system. They require online and remote access, but this is a problem for security officers. Remote online access is considered a major vulnerability which hackers and bad actors can use to penetrate the systems of organizations and individuals. Many companies have stopped or restricted such access. However, mobile technology is becoming more advanced and this access has become a priority for many people, so we will continue to see a push from users to allow it, while it is resisted by security people.

Similarly, countries which are highly connected to the Internet have suffered massive cyberattacks. Those nations with high Internet penetration, where citizens access government services through the Internet, should be extremely concerned about potential cyberattacks launched by state-sponsored or terrorist groups. Such attacks can and will paralyze the services that affect the daily lives of their citizens.

THE CASE OF ESTONIA AND GEORGIA

Estonia is considered to be one of the most Internet-connected countries in Eastern Europe. The use of the Internet in private and governmental agencies and amongst the general population is ranked at the same level as the United States and South Korea. In 2007, many servers in the country were attacked by the DDoS (Distributed Denial of Service) virus, which affected a large number of services, including online banking, government websites and utilities. The public could not access these services; they were out of order. DDoS attacks are considered somewhat benign, since they only cause servers hosting websites to be flooded and jammed with requests coming through email or access requests. When the memory and storage capacities of websites exceed the limits, the system will either perform abnormally or shut down. That is when the operators get involved and resolve the situation. Most of these cyberattacks are carried out by programed centralized computer servers, which hijack computers and turn them into zombies. DDoS viruses are programmed to hit specific operating programs. One primary virus used by these robotic computers is the Botnet virus, which instructs these robotic computers to attack other computers.

If someone's computer becomes a zombie, they do not know about it. They will just notice that the computer is not running at its usual speed. The worm is typically activated as the system is turned on and it takes over the operating system, sending all kinds of requests to other targeted computers and slowing down machines. They can, however, cause huge disturbance to services and are able to shut down websites and block access to computer networks on which many online services are dependent, such as banks, airlines, travel agencies and others.

In Estonia, a huge number of computers were affected, possibly in the thousands. In fact, a major bank was so severely hit that it had to suspend services, in addition to its communication network systems. Estonia blamed Russia, especially since the machines which performed the cyberattacks came from Russian territory. Russia, as usual, denied such action and blamed it on activists and rogue hackers. When conflict erupted between Georgia and Russia, similar DDoS attacks disrupted many Georgian websites and communication infrastructures.

The DDoS attacks on Estonia and Georgia affected their communication systems and impacted the ability of the two countries to communicate within their borders and abroad. NATO stepped in and created for its nation state members a new policy called the

NATO Cyber Defense Policy. In 2008, it also established the Cyber Defense Center in Tallinn, the capital of Estonia. NATO's cyber center does regular exercises with all its partner countries to simulate attacks and find better ways to protect members' infrastructures against cyber threats. A large number of specialists from different countries are involved in testing and improving the Cyber Defense Policy. NATO itself was attacked by hackers who were able to block its website and deny email access to users for several days.

NATO has become aggressive in combating cyber threats. At the NATO summit in Lisbon, members agreed to a new security concept and framework and came up with a cyber defense policy to counter hostile attacks and take immediate protective action. NATO also established the Computer Incident Response Center and Cooperative Cyber Defence Center of Excellence in Tallinn to provide training in cyber threats and protection.

FAKE AND BAD WEBSITES

The World Wide Web (WWW) has been described as a jungle. Millions of websites are not real and are created with the intention of defrauding people. These websites created by bad actors can be so professionally designed and look so believable that it is extremely difficult to distinguish the real from the fake.

There are many ways to tell that a website is fake, but many people lack the time to make the necessary efforts to do so, or do not possess enough technical knowledge. The tools available to hackers and bad actors enable them to clone any website, regardless of whether the register name (domain name) is protected legally. Harvesting the credentials of users (identification and passwords) is a common practice and, in recent years, harvesting financial and banking information has been the ultimate profitable practice of criminal hackers with financial motives.

Fake news has also played a major role in shaping political and social trends in many countries, where it is published on fake websites and fake social media accounts. Facebook and other social media have come under severe attack after accounts have been opened by bad actors in order to sway public opinion and impact countries' elections. This trend is likely to continue and the Internet is the platform for fake news.

The Internet is here to stay and will play a major role in the daily lives of all kinds of users. We have to be ready to face the reality that the cyberattacks of bad actors will multiply in the years to come. Governments, organizations and individuals have to be prepared to face the negative consequences of being connected to and totally dependent upon the Internet. Groups of hackers are becoming smarter with the aid of advanced technical tools which give them easy access to systems, so that Internet security and protection will be playing catch up game. These bad actors will always be one step ahead of the authorities, manufacturers and application developers in finding vulnerabilities and weaknesses that can be exploited.

CHAPTER 8

Famous Cyberattacks

In this chapter, we will discuss the ten most famous cyberattacks that have taken place in recent years. These attacks have had a significant impact on countries, companies and individuals. There have been, of course, more than just ten. In fact, hundreds of similar attacks take place each day, but unfortunately, are either not reported or, if published, mentioned only briefly by the media. These ten cyberattacks have been chosen since it is important that readers understand their impact. The selection is based on research undertaken and two books written by the author. They will shed light on how such attacks can influence and shape targets' views when it comes to cybersecurity issues. The description will not be highly technical, although there are, of course, technical specifications that can be described in detail, but that is not for this book. Readers can do further research in order to understand all the technical aspects of such attacks.

IRANIAN NUCLEAR FACILITY AND STUXNET

The first publicly known cyberattack by one nation on another was Stuxnet. It was a widely reported virus attack and it was confirmed that it was the work of a country or group of nations. Stuxnet was launched to damage and slow down Iranian nuclear facilities, preventing Iran from coming close to developing nuclear technology and, ultimately, atomic bombs. The virus was installed to control units in charge of the spinning of the reactors that enrich uranium at the Natanz uranium enrichment facility. The attack was reportedly a covert operation initiated by the Bush administration to install virus switches controlling these enrichment units and thereby slow down the overall process and/or sabotage the program. Iran admitted that such sabotage had taken place and consequently punished many people involved in operating the nuclear facility. They were considered to be spies working with Western countries.

Stuxnet is considered to be one of the most sophisticated viruses to have been developed. As one looks closely into the structure of the virus code and its functionality, it is apparent that the worm was developed by an organization which was well funded. It required many hours of labor and sophisticated programming. Some reports have suggested that it was the joint work of the United States and Israel. The virus was possibly sent via a computer network or the Internet. For it to have any success, it had to be downloaded using an email system with a file attachment containing the virus. It could launch into any storage device, and particularly USBs (thumb or flash drives), which means that it had to have been an inside job by someone within the facility.

Stuxnet is a time bomb virus, infecting switches that control the spinning of cylinders that enrich uranium. Reports state that Siemens switches used at the Iranian nuclear facility could have already been affected by many zero-day viruses with or without the manufacturer's knowledge and have been activated at a particular time. The virus is programmed to look for and aim at frequency converter drives. These drives control the spinning speed of the centrifuges by altering their speed and ultimately damaging them. Facility operators would not notice changes to the operational rate shown on monitors and operations would appear to be normal. The virus had one mission, which was to slow and damage the centrifuge enrichment controllers. Therefore, it had a limited purpose. It could not spread to other computer devices as other well-known viruses do, which we have presented as examples in this book. It is not known if this virus had any fail-safe mechanism or self-destructive code. What is known is how effective it was in disrupting and damaging the industrial infrastructure of a nation. Stuxnet became known for achieving its objective, damaging approximately 60% of the centrifuges at the nuclear facility, thereby hampering Iranian efforts to come close to being a nuclear nation.

There are many theories about how the Stuxnet virus got into Siemens's control units. The most likely scenario is a USB drive being inserted into a local desktop computer by someone working inside the facility. Another possibility is that an email was sent to a staff member working there. When the staff member opened the attachment file containing Stuxnet, the virus was launched. Stuxnet was coded with a zero-day exploit located within the Windows operating system. It was programmed to infect Windows computers with Step 7 software, SCADA (Supervisory Control and Data Acquisition) and PLC (Programming Logic Controller), which is a hardware device controlling centrifuges for any industrial system.

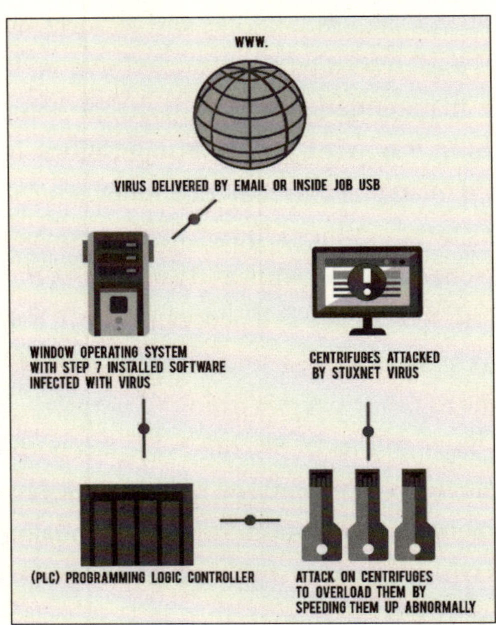

The Stuxnet virus has many layers and it aims at the Windows Operating System, taking advantage of zero-day weakness (Windows claims it has fixes already in place). It targets industrial control systems such as Siemens PCS 7, WinCC and STEP 7 Industrial Software Applications running Windows. Although this worm caused the intended damage, Microsoft found out about the weakness in its software operating system and collaborated with Siemens to develop the right patch, hoping that this fix would stop further hacking. The Stuxnet virus was discovered in June 2010, but several reports indicate that the virus launch may have taken place as early as 2009.

Stuxnet is so sophisticated and complicated that only a nation with advanced technological means could have written the program. The virus contains 500KB (a half megabyte) of codes, and this is considered very large within one application. Its purpose was not to carry out a single attack but multiple attacks simultaneously. The attackers had a thorough knowledge of what to target and when, as well as a good understanding of Windows operating systems, applications and weaknesses. Stuxnet was a worm which kept itself in stealth mode, undetected by the attacked nation. It kept doing its intended job for an extended period until the job was done. Iran only realized something was wrong with its operations in the very late stages, after the damage had already taken place.

Stuxnet codes target vulnerabilities in the processing of files and Windows task schedulers as well as Windows XP. The virus can carry out multiple attacks. It has a program within a master program to carry out a remote exploit using printer spooler subsystems by sending the virus to other peers within the network. There are four Windows zero-day exploits in Stuxnet. One strength of this virus is to ensure that no visible indications of an attack have taken place. There was no memory corruption. It has stealth capabilities, which means the virus is hidden within other programs and is only activated when a zero-date is activated.

Furthermore, Stuxnet used original signature certification, which is required when carrying out any modification or insertion of any executable rootkit programs within the Windows operating system. The attacking nation managed to obtain legitimate certification from two companies authorized by Windows, JMicron and Realtek, both located in Taiwan. Only countries with powerful technological capabilities could accomplish this. The attackers were also able to find out about all the inherent vulnerabilities of Windows, which operates 90 percent of personal computers used in industrial and large and complex computing environments. It is also evident that the attacking nation would have in its arsenal other stealthy viruses, ready to be launched in future attacks. It is a frightening scenario for many countries, which fail to consider this fact when procuring and implementing software systems and applications. They are unaware that the systems have already been infected and vulnerability built into them. In this way, worms and viruses can be unleashed upon any country when desired.

Stuxnet accomplished its mission of damaging nuclear uranium enrichment cylinders, slowing down considerably the Iranian progression towards atomic capabilities. The nations which initiated the attack (always denied by countries accused of such attacks) built identical models of the facility operations, to practice taking control remotely of the plant's activities. Israel reported that it had developed a model for such an attack on its nuclear facility as a dry run to ensure success.

Stuxnet was able to report exactly what was going on within the nuclear facility to two command and control centers in Malaysia and Denmark. It was written in such a smart way that not only was it doing the job it was intended for, but it presented a lie or different reality to technicians and operators working in the nuclear plant. Stuxnet showed them that operations were proceeding normally, when it was just the opposite. The virus issued false reports about the status of center fusion rotation levels. Stuxnet managed to change this rotation to various higher and lower speeds, until it was out of control and ultimately damaging it. However, reports to the plant's operators showed that centrifuges were moving at an average speed. The best part of this Stuxnet virus was that it allowed the attacker nations to keep updating the virus with further instructions and new codes remotely.

Spy agencies can install viruses and worms in computer devices or phones and copy everything or listen to calls made within a certain distance. Listening and monitoring technologies are often used, such as listening posts, relay microwaves and satellite technology. Many cyber technologists discount the possibility of remotely controlling the industrial facilities of another nation. After this and other cyberattacks, Iran decided to invest billions of dollars into its cyber warfare program. Many other nations have also created cyber centers, investing billions of dollars in the hope of defending and protecting industrial and other vital infrastructures.

Windows and other American technology products cannot be sold to Iran, so how they ended up in the plant remains a mystery. It is also surprising that the Iranians chose to use them in an important secret industrial complex, which the world was watching, including major industrial powers like the United States and Israel. They are among a number of nations wishing to stop Iran from becoming a nuclear power.

MIDDLE EAST: DUQU, FLAME AND DDoS

Cyberattackers use these viruses for spying purposes. Both the Flame and Duqu viruses are reported to be the work of nation states because of their advanced technical capabilities and similarity in code writing to Stuxnet. They remain in systems in stealth mode and nations may not know of their existence for many years. Targeted Middle Eastern countries did not report any attack and they were exposed by international reporting. GCC countries, which are considered wealthy, suffered the most. Fingers pointed towards the USA and Israel as the collaborating nations in writing the codes of these two viruses, which are similar in size to Stuxnet, but have a different objective. They were launched to collect sensitive information about industrial and government facilities in Middle Eastern countries.

1. Duqu

This worm was discovered in 2011 and is so-called because some of its files contain the prefix "dq". Its primary purpose is to spy and collect information on targets. The worm is in stealth mode and therefore its codes do not cause any harm to the target's information base and computing records. It is delivered through spearhead phishing attacks. Targets receive emails with attached files and are enticed to open the word document attachments. The email is written in a language familiar to the recipient and does not raise suspicions. When the word document is opened, the worm is launched and immediately exploits the kernel vulnerability of the Windows operating system, mainly the file win32.sys. It remains active, even when the target closes the file. It stays in the computer memory and keeps working in the background, installing itself as a backdoor through which the attacker can enter. It introduces itself as an executable file in the rootkits of the operating system. To be installed, it must use a valid certificate from a digital signatory authority. The companies who provided the licenses were based in Taipei, Taiwan. When the worm takes control of the computer system, it starts to collect information on the system in an incredibly detailed way, even down to the keystrokes. It is so advanced in spying techniques that it can capture screenshots, collect passwords and search for files. Many other functions that we do not know about could include spying on all connected computers, spreading the worm to other computers within the networked facility, like Stuxnet.

In terms of reporting, the Duqu worm can send all collected information to servers located in other countries via telecommunications. Once a nation discovers the existence of this sophisticated and powerful worm, anti-viruses and intrusion detection methods are employed to stop it, but there are always ways to tweak and add more functionality and utilize new vulnerabilities, in order to relaunch it. Presumably, this worm and many others are not only privately owned within industrial countries' military commands but are also available on the black market to anyone who can pay the right price.

2. Flame

In 2012, Aramco Saudi Arabia and RasGas Qatar suffered cyberattacks by a worm called Flame. Aramco and RasGas are both major national oil and gas producing companies for their respected countries. Flame was so infectious that it impacted thousands of computers and it took the companies many weeks to clean up the mess and bring computing operations back to a state of normality. The ultimate damage is not fully known, as these government-owned companies are not allowed to issue press releases or publicly admit that they were targets of cyberattack. There was certainly financial damage, but also a loss of reputation, since they were not able to sustain computing operations. It is well known that these two companies had invested heavily in their computing and telecommunications infrastructures and installed the required firewalls and intrusion detection programs, and updated anti-viruses. Yet with all the human and financial resources at their disposal, they were still unable to stop the virus attack on their systems. The Flame attacks on Aramco impacted approximately 30,000 computers within the company and the damage to RasGas was similar. It is not clear who launched Flame or which country developed it. Iran was one of the countries initially mentioned as the culprit due to its disputes with Saudi Arabia, but we cannot know for sure. Given the sophistication of Flame's code, it is likely that a technologically advanced nation was responsible.

Flame is like other sophisticated worms or viruses which exploit the Windows operating systems. When discovered in 2012, cyber experts found this code extensive and complex; it resembled the code written in Stuxnet. However, the size of the code was found to be higher in format than Stuxnet, which proves that an advanced nation wrote it. It could be from the same country or countries that produced Stuxnet.

The objective of launching Flame was to collect large amounts of information in a mega-data style from targeted companies. The data downloaded from the computing centers and personal computers of the two companies reported was so large that Flame codes contained the functionality of compressing, encryption and transmitting it to cyberattackers' locations internationally. The full capabilities of the Flame worm are not yet known, but there is a certain similarity to Duqu, especially in its spying functionality. Flame is more sophisticated than Duqu. It can record audio and Skype conversations in addition to keyboard activities and traffic. It is able to exploit every vulnerability in the Windows operating systems. Once Flame infects a machine, it is under the attacker's control. The virus can operate remotely, using backdoor commands set up in the rootkits of the operating system. As with other viruses, the cyberattacker needs the authorized digital signatory of the operating system to have the authority to make changes to executable files. Obtaining the private key to allow the cyberattacker to act as the authorized signatory and download files into the kernel's rootkits requires a significant cryptographic ability to copy signatures, because these private keys are typically encrypted. Only the authors of the operating system and associated files are permitted to make any additions or amendments to the existing data in the primary operating system of any computer. The other option to overcome this problem, which is faced by other viruses, is to acquire the original digital signatory authorization from clone companies based overseas in countries such as Taiwan.

The objectives of cyberattackers are still not fully known, but the functionalities of Duqu and Flame indicate that they were for spying. In general, cyberattackers cleverly disguise their attacks through emails written in good English or the language of the country targeted, in this case Arabic. Saudi Arabia Aramco and Qatar RasGas are companies located in two of the wealthiest countries in the GCC. Duqu and Flame were launched through emails which showed a sophisticated knowledge of the oil and gas industry. The email contained a link (rather than an attached file) and when this was clicked on, the worm was launched. The link directed the target to a login page, specially written and designed to gain access to the victim's email, and downloaded files, emails and any other types of data, as per the worm's coded instructions. When using an email approach, which is called spear phishing, the message is reasonable and industry-standard so that the victim will assume it comes from a legitimate source. If the cyberattackers are intelligent, they use personalized emails with specific wording relevant to the field of expertise of the target, whether in the areas of finance, investment, education, healthcare or others, using semantics and terms common within the specific industry.

Cybersecurity officials both at the FBI and FireEye (Cyber Company) identified recent attacks on executives at a number of companies made using a software program called Tor. This program is used by cyberattackers to log into victims' email accounts and route them through the Internet around the globe, thereby making the process of tracking and finding the source of the attacks very difficult for law enforcement officials. These were sophisticated attacks carried out by individuals and most likely organized groups in many different countries. They knew how to write emails in various languages, showing knowledge of the subject, and were able to send them to industries and executives, launching cyberattacks. Flame and Duqu were discovered and patches and fixes to the

Windows operating systems made. However, this does not mean that source codes of these types of worms cannot be modified to avoid detection systems and continue to be launched, achieving their original purposes.

3. DDoS

As mentioned previously, Distributed Denial of Service is what its name implies. The cyberattacker disables the target machine, denying service to its client. This type of virus is so common these days that it is available for hire or sale either through the Internet or on the black market. It has been used by many individuals and groups. In the Middle East, there have been many potentially dangerous attacks targeting the institutions of different countries, made by groups with political agendas or grievances against those countries. Examples of such attacks are the Israeli hackers who attacked the Saudi Stock Exchange (Tadawul). The attack shut down the Stock Exchange's website. Other attacks have included hacking into the websites of different organizations within the Kingdom of Saudi Arabia, such as the attack on the Saudi medical records of students.

Saudi Arabia has also launched cyberattacks upon Israel. For example, a Saudi hacker named OxOmar managed to bring down the Tel Aviv Stock Exchange and El Al airline websites. He also obtained the credit card numbers of many Israeli citizens and published them on the Internet. These cyberattacks continue to happen regularly, in many forms. They are mainly DDoS types of attack. However, worms and viruses with spying and stealth capabilities are also sometimes launched, and these are considered serious threats.

One can expect the numbers of attacks to accelerate in the coming months and years. It is also important to remember that many attacks are never publicly reported due to fear of loss of face and reputation. Those which are reported are therefore just the tip of the iceberg.

SHUTTING DOWN THE WATER SYSTEM IN THE USA

In 2011, a public utility water pump in central Illinois was shut down due to remote hacking. This cyberattack was the first to be reported in the United States media. The perpetrators were foreign and targeted US industrial systems. It is uncertain how the attackers obtained access to the facility. One explanation is that they managed to get credentials with authorization to access the computer network. No one will ever know for sure if it was an inside job or the hackers obtained user access via online hacking. They were able to enter the network's grid without making others aware of their presence and shut down the water facility. Many utility companies use Supervisory Control and Data Acquisition (SCADA) systems. These are specialized software programs which control industrial and facility processes. However, since many industrial facilities require remote monitoring and diagnosis via the Internet, this makes them vulnerable to hacking.

In 2003, a similar attack was made by a worm named the Slammer. It attacked the power grid's network system and electric power was lost in eight states in the North-East of the United States, affecting millions. As a result of these attacks on power and utility grid systems in the United States and globally, many nations, led by the US, asked public and private utility companies to install and operate appropriate cybersecurity systems. The hope was that such systems, protocols and procedures would protect this vital and sensitive infrastructure. It does not mean that these grid systems are safe from cyberattacks just because they have security measures; far from it. The fact is that these systems must connect through the company intranet (which is a network system operating only within the company to connect its computer network systems and employees) and the Internet (which is an open network to everyone outside the company). A hacker can easily penetrate the company's intranet because of its connection to the Internet. The level of damage done depends very much on the type of worm implanted and/or sent out via the Internet. The majority of cyberattacks on power grids come through logic bombs already implanted into computer network systems and software systems which operate power grids, such as SCADA. The fact that logic bombs are already in many systems' networks controlling power grid operations is a worrying scenario for any country.

The main issue here is what nations can do to protect their infrastructure when countries with technological muscle work to weaken their rivals to achieve a specific agenda. Cyberattacks regularly occur amongst the big superpowers and many of the G20 countries meet periodically, discussing how to reduce cyberattacks. However, they do not reveal to each other the cyberattacks they perform secretly, and even if they get caught and evidence is produced pointing to the guilty party, it is always denied, and blame passed on to supposed rogue hackers. The USA and China have been at the center of much controversy in recent times, with attacks generated from both sides. However, official spokespeople always deny the attacks, to escape responsibility and avoid further embarrassment. Cybersecurity is such a serious issue between these two nations that neither will allow companies working in computing and communications networking systems to bid for or obtain contracts with government entities. Many sizeable Chinese telecommunications firms selling computing products and technologies are prohibited from entering into any tender or agreement with United States government agencies, for fear that they will steal or damage the country's sensitive data. Similarly, China does not allow American computer and telecommunications companies to filter into the echelon of Chinese government establishments for fear of spying. Recently, China has taken an even harder line and will now only install locally made computer hardware and software that has been modified and cleansed from any security threats by its government agencies.

A few years ago, the United States had separate cyber command centers in the Army, Navy and Air Force. Recently, they were joined together under one US Cyber Command. Similarly, in 2002 China announced the establishment of the Cyber Warfare Unit; while in 2003, Russia created FAPSI (Federal Commission for Government Communications and Information). Around 20 or more nations have such centers, including France, Israel, Iran, South Korea, India and Pakistan. They all have defensive and offensive capabilities, enabling them to plant cyber weapons, mainly trapdoors and logic bombs, in major computing infrastructures. While some of these centers have carried out cyber espionage and intelligence gathering, others have engaged in cyber espionage against other intelligence agencies, in defiance of local and international regulations and rules. It is a natural process to move from a defensive cyber approach to an offensive one if the country has devoted resources, either human or financial, to cyber warfare. Worms and viruses are available for a reasonable price from the black market, and it is easy for any country to recruit and train programmers and cybersecurity specialists who can create worms and viruses to be used offensively against other nations.

THE WANNACRY CASE

In 2017, hackers launched the WannaCry virus from an unknown location. It attacked Ukraine first, and soon infected many other countries. According to an article in the New York Times, after hacking took place into the NSA (National Security Agency) of the United States, several highly sophisticated hacking tools, viruses and worms were stolen and made available to the highest bidders in the hacking community and the world at large, in 2016. WannaCry could have been one of these stolen viruses. The NSA did not confirm whether this was the case; of course, they would not. A hacking group named the Shadow Brokers claimed responsibility for the attacks. The NSA warned that there would be further attempts at similar hacking globally in the future.

The Shadow Brokers took credit for stealing a cache of exploits, zero-day vulnerabilities and hacking tools from the US National Security Agency. It was ironic that the hackers themselves were hacked. The Shadow Brokers announced that the stolen items were for sale to the highest global bidder.

The WannaCry ransomware took the world of computing by storm. Companies and corporations were affected, as well as the vital infrastructure of many countries, such as hospitals and schools. Zero-day vulnerabilities were exploited in a manner typical of a cyber war between nations. The problem is that when a national security agency of a country maintains an arsenal of viruses and worms used in times of war, the ability of hackers to get to them so quickly opens the door for the highest bidder to obtain them, before using them to launch a cyber war against another country with which they are at odds.

The exploits of the WannaCry ransomware were found in the operating system of Windows XP. Any new version of this operating system was not affected, since a patch to cover the zero-day vulnerability was released, and if implemented, the chances were that the computer would not be affected. The majority of the affected computers showed a message stating that if the amount of money in bitcoin, which is a secure digital means of payment, was not transferred to the account specified by the hackers, then all the files and documents would be lost. The virus managed to encrypt, and there was no way to open the files again unless the amount was transferred. A key for decryption was sent to the victim's computer, to be unlocked. If payment was not made within the specified time frame, then the computer system would shut down permanently and all files and documents would be entirely lost forever. The computer unit would be considered worthless. A solution to the problem was discovered by accident by a British hacker who found a kill switch, which the hackers had implanted into their codes to be able to stop the spread of the virus, and it was used extensively, thereby saving millions of computers from attacks.

In addition, many nation states launch viruses and worms in stealth mode, so they are hidden in library files in operating systems and it is difficult to locate them using anti-virus programs. There are no anti-viruses and firewalls capable of preventing such hidden viruses and worms being launched in the future.

No one knows how hackers managed to improve on the WannaCry virus stolen from the National Security Agency. One imagines that they examined the coding system of the virus in detail and added other tools, such as collecting credentials. Having obtained users' credentials, hackers could use them for future attacks.

The impact of the WannaCry virus cannot be accurately measured, since many cases of hacking are not published for legal and other reasons. Reporting operational incidents or shutdowns of companies impacts profitability. Some institutions cover up hacking incidents and state publicly that they experienced merely "technical problems" and the matter will be resolved soon.

THE ATTACK ON THE QATAR NEWS AGENCY (QNA)

According to media and government statements, the cyberattack on the Qatar News Agency (QNA) took place on May 24th, 2017, but this is not the real date. That is the date of the release of a fabricated voiceover of the Amir of Qatar's speech at a military cadet ceremony on May 23rd. No one knows how long this attack had been planned and when the fake voiceover was delivered to the computer server of QNA.

On May 23rd, 2017, the Amir of Qatar had given a speech, but the broadcast was on May 24th, the next day, on the QNA. The real speech was completely different from the broadcast one, in which the Amir stated that Qatar does not have a good relationship with

President Trump, Hamas is the legitimate representative of the Palestinian people and Iran is a significant power in stabilizing the region. What was striking was that the work had to have been done by professionals with a high level of technical expertise, only feasible in a state-sponsored operation.

The planning of the operation must have been done secretly during the months before the Riyadh Islamic Summit (May 20th-21st 2017). The ultimate objective of the four countries responsible (Bahrain, Egypt, Saudi Arabia and the UAE) was the blockade of Qatar by sea, air and land, potentially leading, if necessary, to actual war and invasion of the country. Qatar was indeed labeled a terrorist country and the four countries declared a total blockade on it. Strangely enough, this included not only trade, but also all relationships between people living in these countries with Qatar.

US media suggested that the hacking was planned and implemented with the approval of the United States of America and President Trump himself.

The details of how this attack was carried out can only be assumed; however, what is known is that carrying out this attack required extensive planning, as well as a thorough knowledge of the computing environment of the agency and the people working there. The hackers had to know the different types of hardware and software applications used, the defense mechanism in place, including firewalls and anti-viruses, and any intrusion and detection tools at the site of the central server. The plan was designed and implemented by one of the four countries which later blockaded Qatar. Those four countries are not equal in technological skills when it comes to hacking activities. Only one country was capable of carrying out the operation and this is the United Arab Emirates. This has now been confirmed by a number of national newspapers, in particular "The Washington Post", which quoted US intelligence as saying that the UAE orchestrated and carried out the hacking on the QNA. The paper even elaborated and stated that many senior members of the

UAE government had planned and carried out the release of the fabricated tape. For its part, senior officials in the Qatari government denied that such remarks were made by the His Highness The Amir Sheikh Tamim bin Hamad Al Thani and declared that QNA had been hacked. Qatar called upon the FBI and Interpol, and both organizations confirmed that it was a case of hacking, but the four countries ignored these facts and the official statements of Qatar and proceeded with their agenda and plan.

Spear phishing is typically carried out through exploiting a weak link in the target victim's armoury. In the case of the QNA, this was remote access to the central server allowed to certain users. The hacker had to identify an individual with remote access and the type of device used, either mobile phone or laptop. In this case, it was probably an iPhone or a Samsung mobile device. As mentioned previously, spear phishing works when users click on a link sent to them by hackers, thereby downloading a virus or worm. The hacker's objective is to move from the mobile device to the central server and take control of it. The worm will collect passwords, including the administrative passwords of a server, thus taking control of the computing environment. This is what happened with the QNA.

Furthermore, the worm can create backdoor capabilities. In other words, the cyberattacker can re-enter the QNA server anytime. It can also generate the ability to feedback, copy and control remotely from another country what is happening within the QNA computing environment, in stealth mode, without the QNA staff being aware of it. The success of the attack was not due to the QNA's lack of technical capabilities, but because of the superior technical ability of the UAE in cyberattacks. The UAE government was able to purchase new viruses and worms from a third party and the black market and it has established working relationships with third party groups of hackers in order to carry out current and future cyberattacks.

The Qatari Ministry of the Interior stated that the IP address(es) from which the attack was made belonged to one of the blockade countries, which is the primary evidence which could be used in any legal claim about other countries' involvement. These IP addresses are Internet protocols with specific numbers belonging to cyberattackers' devices. If they were used to send the link with the worm attached in a file to the individual targeted within the QNA, then the scenario of the attack described above is correct. The UAE has had business dealings with companies with links to Israel. An Israeli company called NSO (mentioned earlier in this book) has sold its mobile hacking tools to many nations, including the UAE, for espionage purposes. These tools are expensive and they vary from one mobile device to another. Other companies with links to Israel have also been involved in assisting the UAE to build its hacking capabilities, as reported in the media.

This kind of cyberattack has already been denounced as illegal, and under international law it is criminal. The countries involved must be held liable and face prosecution. However, there are problems with making a clear case against those responsible and governments will deny direct involvement, claiming that the attacks were carried out by a third party or groups or individuals who sympathize with particular governments. Legal responsibility might be in doubt. However, with accurate forensic and technical facts, a case against the UAE could be established. Given recent reports by the respected American newspaper, "The Washington Post", it seems highly likely that the UAE government was involved. The UAE's foreign minister and ambassador to the USA, Yousef Al-Otaiba, has denied this. The ambassador himself was a victim of a spear phishing attack following the QNA attack, for which a group using GlobaLeaks software claimed responsibility. The hackers managed to take control of the laptop of the ambassador and copied all his files and emails. Some of the emails were released on websites and leaked to international media, thereby exposing UAE efforts to influence events in Washington and around the region.

SONY

Sony International USA witnessed one of the most significant cyberattacks on any corporation in modern times. In 2012, Sony's PlayStation network system was shut down by hackers. Approximately 100 million accounts with personal information stored on the company's computer system were compromised. This cyberattack caused not only a loss of confidence in Sony's security system, but it also showed hackers' ability to penetrate and download all types of sensitive information. Sony did not just lose financially; it also lost its reputation and the confidence of its loyal customers.

Two years later, in 2014, another attack turned out to be even more damaging. This time, the target was Sony Entertainment, based in Los Angeles, California. It produces major blockbuster movies. This attack on the computing environment of the company was considered so severe that not only was the public alarmed, but even politicians took notice. The President of the United States of America commented on the seriousness of the cyberattack and the damage it caused.

Between these two attacks, the Sony Corporation had spent large sums of money and taken on extra staff to heighten its cybersecurity. It hired major cybersecurity firms to ensure that its computing environment was secure. It installed firewalls, anti-viruses and intrusion detection measures to counter different types of viruses and worms known to the industry. Sony believed that with this strong computing security, cyberattacks were distant possibilities. It turned out to be a wrong assumption and this cyberattack has been described as the worst on any public corporation.

Every major report in the media pointed fingers at North Korea, following the statement of federal authorities. The reason for the attack was that Sony was about to release a new movie called "The Interview" about the assassination of North Korea's president. In the comedy film, two journalists are recruited by the CIA to go to North Korea and achieve the impossible goal of gaining an interview with the country's president and assassinating him.

Federal authorities indicated that Sony's virus was written with a trace of the North Korean language in it. Therefore, it must have been initiated by North Korea with the motive of stopping the release of the new movie which would harm the reputation of the country and its president. North Korea was named as the culprit continuously in media and statements by US government officials. There was no concrete proof from the government's cyber intelligence agencies and reliable sources in North Korea, but a culprit was needed. For now, it is the only suspect. What was the damage done to Sony? Early reports state that cyberattackers managed to extract valuable classified personal information about company staff, including salaries, health care files, passwords, social security numbers and even the value of bonuses given. Attackers also managed to download the newest movies before they were released, which caused future financial losses. They were not satisfied with downloading all of the company's files, videos and other types of information, but also wrote a virus with instructions to wipe clean storage devices and shut down the company's computing environment.

A group calling itself Guardians of Peace with a hashtag (#GOP) claimed responsibility. No one had heard of this group before, nor was it known to which country they belonged. There are many theories as to how the worm was delivered and launched. One assumes that Sony's security measures would have prevented any worm from penetrating its systems and therefore one might assume that it was an inside job, similar to the Stuxnet launch at the Iranian nuclear facility. There were reports that a disgruntled employee managed to insert the worm using a memory stick. It is the most likely scenario. However, media reports kept North Korea's story alive, giving increasing publicity to the "The Interview". Sony was careful not to blame North Korea by name during the investigation.

The immediate effect of the attack on the Sony Corporation was that the entire computing environment shut down and the company had to resort to manual operations and office paperwork. Sony could not even start again by rebooting the system. The worm has still not been identified by either cyber experts or the FBI who were assigned to the case.

After #GOP announced itself as the hacker, it was generally assumed that it was a group supported by North Korea. It was not surprising news to the cybersecurity community. North Korea has some capabilities, and with the help of the Russians and Chinese, it can launch cyberattacks globally. It has over 700 cyber programmers who are not necessarily stationed in North Korea but could be in China or Russia. The government of North Korea denied the attack, blaming it on sympathizers and supporters of the country against the intention of Sony to launch the movie, which was causing extreme embarrassment to the President of North Korea. One newspaper claimed that the group initiated the attack from a hotel lobby in Thailand, which had public WiFi. This story, which lacked any proof, immediately died. It is well known that to attack a protected computing facility, especially at Sony, the attack would have to be made from a sophisticated environment, not a hotel lobby. Following the attack, the movie "The Interview" was released and DVD copies were distributed all over the world. Everyone knew it was a comedy with a scenario only Hollywood could think up and not a serious attack on North Korea. However, the main issue here is about the hacking of Sony and why it could not stop the attack, given all the cyber protection measures in place.

In recent cases, the goals of cyberattacks vary from stealing files and sensitive information, to disruption of computing network environments. The motive behind such action is either malicious or financial. In the Sony attack, the intention was not only to steal, download and publish files, but to destroy all the information stored on drives by wiping them clean. This type of action is considered severe and the most complicated task for any virus or worm launched by a hacking group. Until the writing of this book, the nationality of #GOP (Guardians of Peace), which claimed responsibility for the hacking, has not been revealed.

Sony had managed to back up all the necessary information. Many large companies have duplicate back up facilities to restore operation in times of disaster. We can only hope that when the backup took place, programs and applications were copied. In large corporations such as Sony, it is unproductive, time-consuming and frustrating for employees and company officials to have their emails made public and to be unable to get back to computing operations immediately. No doubt the cybersecurity company or companies hired to clean up the infection of the worm worked diligently to restore computing operations as soon as possible. It is not impossible that the worm or virus is in stealth mode, awaiting future activation instructions to come alive and be re-launched, following the restoration of computing operations at Sony. One major remaining issue is how we can ensure that a worm is not still dormant on personal computers, given that the virus has not been identified and there is no anti-virus toolkit for it. The fastest way to restart operations is to install new computers and a network system from scratch, which could be expensive, in the hope that the back-up system of the company is not infected and there is no repeat of this unfortunate and devastating episode. The United States government and even the President of the United States of America, Barack Obama, came out publicly and labeled the attack as cyber war, which is unusual and unprecedented coming from an American president. In a public news appearance, he assured the American people that the United States would take appropriate action at the time of its choosing. North Korea, on the other hand, responded publicly and denied vehemently that the attack had come from its country and people. North Korea requested the United States to produce any evidence it had and requested that a team be established to work jointly on this matter. The NSA and

FBI did not disclose any detailed information on the attackers but briefed government officials and the President about the strong evidence they had collected, which according to them pointed to North Korea as the originator of the attacks. They claimed North Korea has used similar worms and viruses in cyberattacks on South Korea, where the data of many computers has been wiped clean after information has been downloaded from them, and these computers have become inoperable.

The Sony attack is the first one made allegedly by a country against a large media company based in the USA. It caused financial damage to the company and political damage to the USA. In a televised interview, the Sony CEO confirmed that the attack could not be stopped even with the most robust firewall and advanced cybersecurity the company possessed. The CEO emphasized that the company had recruited very specialized cybersecurity people and, in fact, was working closely with the authorities, especially the FBI, following previous attacks.

The United States, meanwhile, requested that the Chinese government block any cyberattacks from North Korea. This was a bizarre request, given the fact that the relationship between the two countries was strained, after the United States had accused China of responsibility for cyberattacks on U.S. companies. The U.S. government had named five high ranking Chinese military officials by name and splashed their pictures all over the media, which caused embarrassment to China. The U.S. asked for cooperation from China to block any networking access to North Korea, since the North Korean telecommunications network is handled by the Chinese web and must go through its telecommunications network system to the outside world. The company in China handling all the Internet traffic of North Korea is the China United Network Communications Group, better known as China Unicom. This is why it seems unlikely that North Korea would have been able to carry out the attack, despite its strong reasons for doing so. The incident caused many companies to go on high alert, having realized how easy it was for hackers to shut down the entire infrastructure of a company.

Sony's computer networks and all of its files and data were wiped out after they had been downloaded from the computer hard drives. Approximately 100 terabytes of the company's data was displayed to the public for all to see. It caused severe embarrassment not only to the executives of Sony but all their employees and families, since personal email exchanges and conversations with movie stars and others became public. The cost of the attack, according to the Sony CEO, was incalculable. "The Interview", which had caused all the controversy, cost the company approximately 75 million dollars. Sony claimed that movie theaters around the country refused to show the movie for fear of being attacked. According to the CEO, the company intended to release it in the United States through digital video or online on-demand movies. The overall financial damage due to the attack may have been over 500 million dollars.

In his press conference, Barack Obama stated that the United States was planning to take offensive action against the infrastructure of North Korea, in response to the attacks. Such a retaliatory attack would involve the use of DDoS (Distributed Denial of Service), where the Internet network of North Korea would be flooded with packets of data so massive that the country would be partially if not completely shut down. North Korea has only 1024 Internet protocol addresses, not as many as a small city in the United States, which might have thousands. As such, the country has one of the lowest Internet penetration rates in the world. It is an intranet networked nation, ie. the network within the country is controlled by a state-owned company through which the state directs online activity via a communications setup within China. So, all Internet traffic is routed through the Chinese National Network System. After Obama's warning, there was disruption to Internet facilities in North Korea. No-one knows for sure what caused it. Did it come from the North

Korean government itself trying to block its Internet from the outside world, fearful of a potential attack from the United States government or groups associated with the government? Or was it an attack by the United States? Of course, the United States would not be directly involved in a cyberattack. Rather, it would finance a third party to carry out the attack, which is the game regularly played by governments around the world.

Following the attack on Sony, many cyber specialists waited anxiously to learn about the type of worm used and to find out details of the writing of the code that caused such massive damage, and whether it was an inside job or an attack carried out through the World Wide Web. An inside job is most likely. Such an attack would have been difficult to carry out over the Internet, given its sophistication. However, if it is proven that this cyberattack was indeed generated by North Korea and that the country sponsored the GOP (Guardians of Peace) to carry it out, the case will be unprecedented because the attack came from a country which has very low Internet penetration. Despite being a nuclear nation, it is not technically advanced. This makes one wonder what countries with technological muscle and a political or financial grudge could do if they wished to harm other nations. As oil prices slide from a high of 110 dollars per barrel to less than 60 dollars within a few weeks or months, Russia and other countries will feel these financial losses and may start to blame other nations. Potential retaliation could be in order, and we do not know what the future holds. Ultimately, we know that nations will resort to any means to protect their national interests, and they will view the loss of future revenues as an act of war.

ANTHEM INCORPORATED

There have been media reports of many similar cyberattacks on large corporations across the USA, although the FBI and other law enforcement agencies in the United States have not revealed details of the results of their investigations. The only information provided has been in press releases issued by public relations departments. For example, a serious corporate cyberattack took place on the number two American health insurer, Anthem Incorporated. 80 million records were stolen from a database belonging to the company, one of the worst attacks on a health insurance company. The data taken was personal information related to consumers and employees. The stolen records had value on the black market. Even though they were medical records, they contained useful sensitive information. The attack was so sophisticated that it could not have been completed successfully unless the perpetrator was another country with advanced cyber technology. The United States, as usual, named China as the culprit.

Anthem reported the cyberattack incident immediately, due to fear of being sued. Other companies in similar situations typically would not. The company contacted the FBI and claimed that the security breach in its IT system had been fixed and security was restored. One might wonder if there was any cybersecurity before this incident happened. We assume there were extensive security measures taken, given the recent hacking of corporate America, but this could not prevent cyber hacking into one of the biggest corporations in the United States.

Other corporations have been attacked, such as Home Depot, from which 53 million email addresses were stolen. Target was also hit and 70 million customers' records taken. However, the Sony cyberattack is considered the most brazen and damaging, and it used one of the most sophisticated worms ever written to attack a major corporation. These types of cyberattacks will continue as long as advanced hackers have the technical ability to carry them out. We can therefore expect to hear more such news in the future, although some attacks will be reported and others not.

YAHOO

This company is one of the largest free email account providers, serving over 1 billion customers worldwide. In its annual filing in September 2016, the company announced that 500 million user email accounts had been compromised and hacked by an unknown actor, most likely a state-sponsored hacker.

It was one of the largest known data breaches in history. Many media reports suggested that the number of 500 million accounts was inaccurate and the real number was probably close to a billion. Exactly what information was compromised is not known, but certainly it would have included email addresses and personal information of users, such as phone numbers and addresses. Passwords were probably also compromised. Although many large companies encrypt passwords using a technique called hashing, skilled hackers have the methods and tools to decrypt them.

The big question is when did Yahoo find out about the breach? Did they find out when it happened in 2014 and fail to inform the public or later in 2016, when they informed the authorities of the data breach? If it was in 2016, it is incredible that the cybersecurity team did not find out about it before. This would imply that the hacking was state-sponsored, since these kinds of hackers utilize stealth worms to steal data without the knowledge of the targeted victim. State-sponsored hackers are hired by individual states with specific political or other agendas which do not wish to be held directly responsible for the hacking. In the case of Yahoo, reports stated that a group called Group E from an Eastern European country was involved.

How did the hackers manage to access such a large number of accounts? Most email account providers utilize what we call cookies. These cookies are meant to facilitate users' access to their accounts. When a user clicks on the Yahoo logo, the cookie is activated and remembers the log in user identification and password, enabling the user to access the account easily, without re-entering these details. This service is provided to make email account access easier and smoother. However, hackers have found a vulnerability in this process. If they can gain access to the code of the cookie, then it is easy to forge it and present it as the original, enabling them to access the account without the need to obtain a password. The second possibility is that hackers downloaded a worm into Yahoo's central servers and managed to access the database containing all the user identification and password files, thus making it easy to transfer and copy all the accounts.

Why should Yahoo users worry? When a user's email account is stolen and sold to a third party, this account can be utilized in a phishing scam. We have already discussed the phishing technique and how hackers and criminal groups send emails to all contacts listed in the stolen email account in order to defraud recipients into sending money to an account set up by them. It can also be used to obtain other essential credentials, such as banking information, by cloning the website of a bank or other financial institution and requesting the user to re-enter personal banking information. There are many ways in which hackers can utilize a compromised email account.

Yahoo was forced to inform account holders that their email accounts had been compromised and that they would need to change their passwords. It was the only solution. However, if hackers had managed to highjack users' accounts, then there was little chance of accessing those accounts and email communications, unless Yahoo managed to restore them from its backup system.

EQUIFAX DATA BREACH

In September 2017, Equifax, one of the three largest consumer credit reporting agencies, with over 800 million customers, both individuals and businesses, announced a significant breach of the cybersecurity of its databases. Hackers had managed to download millions of accounts of credit card customers. The number of accounts compromised was stated to be in the thousands, but if hackers had managed to collect thousands, then why not all the accounts? These accounts contained personal information, such as names, addresses, social security and driver license numbers and passport information. By March 2018, the total number of affected consumers was identified by Equifax as being over 148 million, that is, approximately half of the population of the USA.

Equifax agreed with the Consumer Financial Protection Bureau to pay $425 million to those affected. However, this amount could not compensate for the fact that customers' personal information had ended up in the hands of a third party who could potentially use it for criminal activities in the future.

How did it happen? Equifax stated that specific vulnerabilities in its website may have enabled hackers to access its database. The website was used by Equifax as an online app portal into which businesses and government organizations could log and report their disputes with the company. Forensic investigators found out that there was a vulnerability in a tool named Apache Struts used by Equifax to build its web applications. Hackers managed to compromise this and gain control of the portal. From there, with an SQL injection, they managed to download and transfer consumer records from the company databases. The vulnerability was patched, but catastrophic damage was already done to the company's reputation as well as consumers.

What damage can a consumer expect when a serious data breach such as this occurs? One primary concern is identity theft. Personal information, as described above, can be used to create fake documents such as passports, social security cards, driver licenses and other essential documentation. Furthermore, there is a strong possibility that email addresses and names in the hands of hackers will be used for phishing activities.

What can a consumer do? Equifax created a website for affected consumers, where they could report damage they had suffered to the company. The company later claimed that it had patched the vulnerability and all consumer records were now safe.

TARGET

Target is the third largest retailer in the USA. In 2013, the company reported that 40 million records of credit and debit cards of its customers had been compromised. This cyberattack impacted customers of 1,797 Target stores in the USA. Hackers managed to steal all the card data, including numbers, PIN and other security codes, and issue dates.

Despite advanced security measures in place to protect the integrity of its databases, Target security specialists were unable to prevent the attack. How did it happen? The hackers used legitimate credentials obtained from a third-party contractor, the HVAC company. This company handles heating and air conditioning for all of Target's retail stores. HVAC had remote access to the computing systems of all the stores and from there it could access the stored data of consumers. This process of entry is a classic one, typical of what can happen when companies use a third party to handle its business. If hackers manage to hack into the third party's systems and if these are connected with the servers and computer network of Target, then every aspect of Target's computing operations is compromised. Obtaining credentials can be done in many ways, including through simple social engineering (explained in later chapters). Third-party contractors working for Target might not have had robust cybersecurity technology. Hackers always look for the weakest point of entry and in this case, they found it.

The effect on Target was, of course, devastating financially and legally, not including the damage to its reputation. The impact on consumers was even greater, considering that their sensitive financial information and personal data was out in public and in the hands of bad actors with an agenda to use it for illegal and criminal activities.

MARRIOTT

In 2018, the Marriot hotel group, which has a number of hotel brands under its umbrella, confirmed that it had suffered a data breach which affected over 500 million of its customers worldwide.

The reservation system containing customer records was hacked. These records included names, email addresses, passport numbers, credit card information, departure and arrival details and other personal information. The hackers managed to download all the records and encrypt them. When Marriott learned of the attack and discovered that its records had been encrypted, it managed to decrypt the data and restore it to its original form.

How did it happen? One possibility is phishing, sending emails and links to employees working within the group's hotels. If they clicked on the links or opened files attached to an email, malicious codes, such as the Trojan Horse, would be downloaded. From there, the worm could obtain employees' credentials and privileged administrative credentials, making it easy for hackers to access the reservation databases.

What impact did it have? For Marriott, it was catastrophic. It resulted in a huge loss of reputation and a hefty fine by the authorities, exceeding one billion US dollars. For consumers, of course, the dangers were identity theft and phishing by hackers. Major newspapers in the USA and government officials claimed that Chinese state-sponsored hackers were responsible for the data breach, which they had carried out in order to collect information on the USA and the customers of other Marriott group hotels.

The solution for this data breach was simply to ask customers to change their passwords to stronger ones, using a three-step authentication process. The hotel group took the necessary steps to increase their cybersecurity protection to stop another attack. However, that will not stop future hacking, since state-sponsored actors have the technological abilities to repeat such attacks if desired.

CHAPTER 9

Wireless Security

Wireless security refers to the type of network system, whether that of an individual, home or business, which can be compromised by unauthorized access.

The term "wireless" typically correlates with WiFi. A primary standard governs wireless systems, especially mobile smartphones and laptops. This is 802.11, a number assigned by the IEEE (Institute of Electrical and Electronics Engineers) with various extensions representing different specifications. It is the standard for WiFi usage for clients sending and receiving messages from a wireless access point, the main point to which mobile and other devices are connected.

There are multiple devices and units (hardware), in addition to the software system, which govern the installation and usage of any wireless system. The server (computer unit) controls such devices, routers and switches, and also portable devices, including mobile phones, tablets and laptops.

Data in the wireless environment is sent and transmitted using radio waves, with different radio frequencies and different throughputs. For example, the SSID (Service Set Identifier) is the name of the wireless network that a user connects to when using public WiFi. They can choose this network from the list of WiFi networks available in that location and other nearby ones. The network administrator chooses the SSID name and allocates it to all users in the location covered by the WiFi. There is also BSSID

(Basic Service Set Identifier), which has the necessary information determining the address of the device connected to the SSID. This MAC (Machine Control Address) reveals the unique serial number of the device when it is connected to WiFi. The station is the client device, whether mobile, laptop or any other smartphone device, that is connected to a wireless network. Finally, there is the access point, which is the primary hardware device used by an establishment or organization to provide WiFi access for clients or customers.

POPULARITY FACTOR

Technology has progressed from desktop workstations to current mobile handsets and small laptops or tablets that have similar powers and capabilities to desktops. A few years back, in order to connect with others by computer and access websites, etc., you had to sit at a desktop connected to a network system or enter the service area of a business where access was provided for a fee. Those years are truly gone, and people are no longer willing to sit for hours in a chair using a desktop. Using the latest mobile and laptop technology is the norm, and there are applications enabling people to order food, taxis and other means of transport, as well as booking hotels. These social media apps are designed for lives constantly on the move. Most places have wireless systems and if there is no access due to password restrictions, people can create their own wireless hotspots hosted by Internet service providers (ISP), the telecommunications companies in each country.

Telecommunications companies (Internet service providers) have realized that the days of high profit margins from telephone calls are in the past, given the various applications in the market providing video, text and voice conversation for a small subscription, or even for free as long as users agree to receive advertisements on their phone screens.

DATA MAGIC

Internet Service Providers (ISP) have realized that the big money will come when billions of people are attracted to a wireless environment where mobility is the key. They can carry their portable devices anywhere as long as there is a wireless environment to enable them to conduct business and provide social connection with other users worldwide. Today's portable devices not only have phone capabilities but also all the technical capabilities of a desktop workstation wired to big computers. The least expensive portable device will have a capacity of 64 Gigabytes of storage and a central processing unit (CPU) working at a speed equivalent to a fixed computer 10-15 years ago. These portable devices can perform all necessary communication and computing-related activities. In fact, there are (more expensive) portable devices with the power of a minicomputer. This is good news for users and it can also be bad, since these portable devices used in a wireless environment are susceptible to hacking and can be compromised in a way that impacts the privacy and integrity of the stored data.

The magic of data has led makers of many portable devices to increase their storage and processing capabilities, enabling companies such as Facebook, Amazon, Google and others to collect massive amounts of data. This would not have been possible without the mobility provided by the wireless environment.

HOW SECURE IS WIRELESS?

The simple illustration below shows that when you use your portable devices in a wireless environment, it does not mean that you are safe from hacking and sniffing of the communication carried out through such devices.

The diagram below shows a simple configuration of a wireless setup, using two portable laptops connecting to an access point (router) and then to the Internet (World Wide Web). A server (computer) unit provides interconnectivity with Internet service providers and necessary storage of data communication (not shown in the picture). This type of configuration can be anywhere – at home, in an office or various wireless locations such as airports, coffee shops, malls, etc.

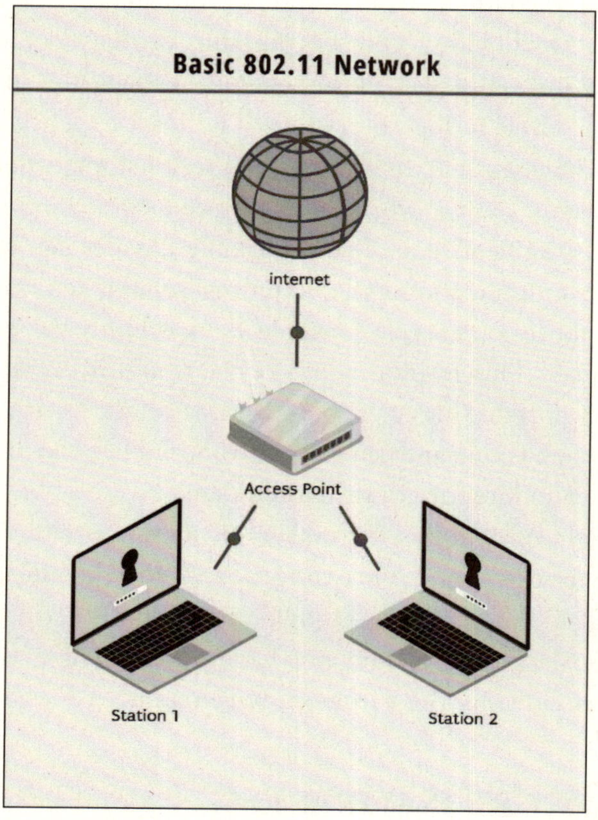

The Figure above shows that if station 1 sends a data packet to the Internet, it sends it first to the access point; then the access point forwards it to the Internet. When station 1 sends a packet to station 2, it must go through the access point and cannot be sent directly to station 2. There is a protocol that governs such communication, either using frequencies or throughputs within a wireless system, and it is called the 802.11. The table below shows the numbers.

Flavors of 802.11

Name	Frequency	Max Throughput
802.11b	2.4 GHz	11 Mbps
802.11g	2.4 GHz	54 Mbps
802.11n	2.4 GHz / 5 GHz	600 Mbps*
802.11ac	5 GHz	866.7 Mbps*

These throughputs are theoretical and represent the maximum speeds possible. However, those actual speeds are not seen.

In the following Figure, we can see how the connection works between a portable device and a wireless system. It is very simple.

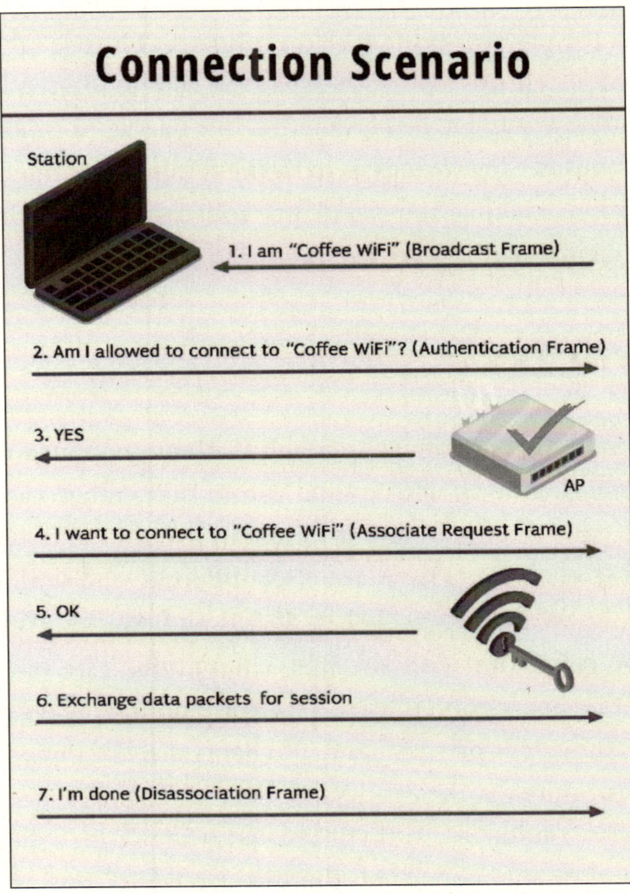

It is important to understand the simple Figure above, since it illustrates that the security of a wireless connection used by a portable device cannot be guaranteed. The connection of such portable devices with routers (Access Points) can be disrupted and compromised. Internet connection becomes the target of hackers and bad actors who rely on insecure communication and being able to access devices, downloading and sniffing data and different types of communication.

There are mechanisms to provide the necessary security, such as passwords and encryption, but when individual users have a number of portable and smart devices connected to the Internet using wireless systems, it is very difficult, and in many cases impossible, to remember the passwords for each one of them. The use of passwords is a means to ensure your access to the wireless environment is secure, but how can you be certain that this password is not going to be compromised? This brings us to the next important subject, which is encryption; making the password and communication of data inaccessible in a wireless environment.

ENCRYPTION

Encryption of WiFi traffic is optional. Without encryption, packets are sent in a clear form and anyone within radio range can listen to them. We can reconfigure our wireless to listen to all packets on a given WiFi channel. There are four different encryption modes available for WiFi: Open, WEP, WPA and WPA2. WPA3 will potentially come out with stronger encryption. The open option means that no encryption is used. The WEP option means that there is "wired equivalent privacy" and all clients use the same key. This is not a safe option.

The WPA option is "WiFi protected access", in which not all clients use the same key. Then there is the WPA2 option which is highly protected and similar to WPA but uses a more advanced ciphering algorithm.

SIMPLE ATTACKS

The following examples show how hackers can typically penetrate and compromise a wireless environment.

1. Forced Disassociation

Control frames, which are messages requesting to connect with WiFi, do not need to be authenticated in any way. Anyone in range with a wireless network card can create control frames claiming to be from anyone. In a simple attack scenario, the hacker will send a large number of disassociation frames (transmission requests) to a client on the network, which will cause a blockage of wireless service. When the association is recreated by the AP, hackers will be able to obtain a victim's credentials, such as their passwords.

2. Traffic Sniffing

If encryption is not used and data is sent unencrypted, hackers will listen and see all the data in plain text, which gives easy access to it.

Simple attack: Listen to all traffic. Look through it for interesting things (passwords, emails and other relevant information).

3. WEP Shared Key

With WEP, all clients use the same encryption key. If one person knows the key, he/she can use it to decrypt the data of people who have joined the network. A key can be broken in a matter of minutes or less. The encryption algorithm has some mathematical problems. In a simple attack, the hacker will listen and decrypt data traffic from other clients easily.

4. WPA Password Choice

WPA lets the user pick a password for an AP. Users tend to pick bad passwords. In a simple attack, brute force will be applied to the WPA password and credentials easily obtained, as the data will be in plain text. Similar techniques of brute force can be used on the encrypted environment when WPA2 is present. However, this might take a long time and will require patience, as well as further tools to uncover passwords.

A hacker can use, for example, the Kali Linux tool (which is popular amongst hackers) on his or her mobile devices to activate a hacking process in a WiFi environment. Hackers typically use laptops when they are in a public WiFi area.

TRAFFIC SNIFFING

This hacking technique, using Kali tools, enables hackers to look deeper into network systems. Network systems are equipped with switches and routers to facilitate successful communication between hosts and users within the network. All traffic generated between hosts at data centers and users connected to hosts must go through these switches or routers. They are like buses or trains, or even better taxis which carry passengers and their luggage from point A to point B. If an email is sent, it has to have a header, which contains all kinds of information: sender, receiver, subject, email address and all other relevant information for the setup protocol of a network device, the OSI (Open System Interface). All traffic communications must abide by this protocol in order for traffic to be sent successfully. Then one has the main body of the email. The email must be carried by the switch or the router. This will know to which address within a local area network the email should be sent. It is similar to the post office running the postal delivery of residents in a town. The switch's job is easy and it sends the email to that address within the local area network (LAN). If a person's computer or device is not turned on, then delivery from the switch point of view has been completed. But if the device receiving the expected email is off, then switches, which are smart machines, keep the email in a mail outbox, waiting for a signal that the device intended to receive the mail has now been turned on, and has acknowledged that it is the correct intended recipient. When this happens, the email is sent. If the recipient of the email is not within the same local area network but in another location or even another country, then electronic delivery will count on the Internet to make the delivery. In this case, smart switches typically will request an assignment of an Internet Protocol address (IP), which is one of the first protocols that governs communications traffic on the Internet.

Each device connected to the Internet must have MAC and IP addresses. The MAC (Media Access Control) is the serial number of the connected device held by hosts that maintain network systems. The MAC consists of a long number. The first half of it represents the manufacturer's identification and the second half is a unique number intended only for that device. As stated, the IP address is an address assigned by the Protocol, and the operating system of the organization can also allocate a numbering system to it. The network administrator can do this for all of the connected devices of staff within an organization, either automatically or manually, and maintain a table for such addresses to refer to when there is data to send.

Given the above brief description of how traffic is generated and sent and what devices and addresses are used, traffic sniffing is one of the necessary early steps that hackers will take. They will look for emails and digital transmission by sniffing into the network's traffic. In the networking world, digital transmission of traffic is called packets. A packet contains all types of information, including but not limited to header, transmitter, recipient, subject, date and main content of the packet. The size of the packet is not important. There is a protocol to organize packet sending, and this is called FTP (File Transfer Protocol). These protocols are necessary for specific layers of communication between two parties to be successful. Without such protocols, communications can fail.

Hackers try to sniff these packets by any means. Some of their methods are as simple as hacking into a house's WiFi, while stationed in a vehicle outside the building, and then using sniffing tools to collect packets transmitted.

If encryption is used on the transmission of packets, then the sniffing task for hackers will be more difficult but not impossible. However, if the traffic is not encrypted, then the task is much simpler.

SPOOFING AND SESSION HIJACKING

This is another kind of attack upon the network system and communications while carrying out traffic sniffing. Hackers can intercept the lines used for connecting to a local telecommunications station and redirect the traffic and packets sent between different parties, while users are completely oblivious of the interference. Emails are sent to hackers rather than their intended recipients.

In conclusion, wireless security is not secure. Portable device users should be aware of many types of potential hacking, as mentioned above. Having a strong password with high encryption can minimize hackers' ability to sniff and highjack data communications, but security is not complete, since hackers with advanced tools are able to compromise wireless connections and obtain data easily.

CHAPTER 10
Identity Fraud and Theft

There is a difference between identity theft and identity fraud. Identity theft means stealing personal information, while identity fraud is the use of this stolen personal information for criminal ends, such as the creation of fake credit cards, employment and travel documents, passports, identification cards and other important credentials. This type of fraud is always short term, since it will be discovered in the long run.

THE OBJECTIVE

We have witnessed incidents of identity fraud in the areas of illegal immigration and smuggling. Criminal groups who have obtained the stolen personal information of victims, fraudulently sell documents such as immigration visas, citizen documents and other types of documents enabling immigrants and travelers to cross borders.

Stolen personal information used in fraudulent activities is big business for criminal groups. There are people who would like to assume someone else's identity in order to escape capture and criminal prosecution or to be able to work. In recent years, even credentials of higher education have been forged in order to obtain work in many countries.

LACK OF REPORTING

There is the perception by many that the loss of personal information is not important and therefore reporting it to the authorities is not a priority unless fraud happens. However, by then it will be too late. When fraud is reported, then the authorities step in to try and capture the culprits, hoping that they are local. However, if the fraud of stolen identity has happened across national boundaries, then the local authority can accomplish little, as there is an issue with legal jurisdictions, given that each country has its own laws regarding identity theft and fraud.

Furthermore, legal authorities of a country where a citizen witnessed an identity theft and potential fraud will have little means legally to pursue bad actors who have obtained an identity from another country. The only option is to report the fraud to that country, in the hope that a cooperation agreement on the matter can be made. This process is a lengthy one and most likely the culprits will never be caught and brought to justice.

LOSS OF PERSONAL INFORMATION

There are many ways in which one's personal information can be stolen and used for fraudulent activities.

1. Traditional Physical Methods

Let us assume you arrive at your favorite hotel and finish checking in, get into your room and unpack your luggage. You decide to leave the room to go down to meet up with your friend in the lobby, leaving your laptop and other digital devices in the room. You come back to your room to find that not only your valuable items such as money, watches and jewelry have been stolen, but also your digital devices such as your laptop.

Now we assume that you placed some of your valuable items in the secure box in your room with the PIN activated. That is safe and no one can access it except you. However, your other items, including your laptop, are missing.

Let us take another situation which occurs so often. You are sitting in a coffee shop and suddenly receive an emergency call that forces you to leave in hurry, forgetting to pick up your mobile device. Or you go shopping and visit many stores but in one of them you leave behind your mobile phone, and you do not remember which one. You go back to the coffee shop or to the stores you shopped in, and salespeople tell you, "Sorry, we cannot locate your phone".

There are many examples like the ones described above. What would it mean to lose your digital devices? It would mean that all your personal information stored in them is potential material for identity fraud.

There are other traditional physical methods such as mail and dumpster diving. When mail and personal documents are thrown in the trash, they can be used by thieves to obtain personal information and then to create fraudulent documents such as credit and identification cards.

2. Card Skimming and ATM Manipulation

These methods are used increasingly by criminal groups to obtain credentials and do not require technical skills. Let us assume you are sitting in a restaurant with friends and family having dinner. When the time comes to pay with your credit card, you give your card to the waiter, who can find out your PIN by one of two methods. He can take your card back to the paying station and insert it into a card reader which skims all the information stored on it. Or he uses the authentic card reader and you enter your personal PIN. Even if that personal PIN is not skimmed or read by an illegal machine, your fingerprints on the authentic credit card machine can be read under infrared, showing your PIN.

Fake ATMs are another popular method used by criminal groups. Masks resembling the real face of the ATM are placed over the machine. A victim entering credit card details for transaction purposes such as money withdrawal or payments in a gas station would not notice the difference, since all that happens is that the credit card is rejected or a message appears, saying that the ATM is out of service. The mask over the real face of the ATM contains a credit or ATM card reader which skims all the personal information stored on the card and even has online capabilities to transfer data to criminal locations.

The hardware units of card skimmers and ATM manipulation devices are sold on the Internet and obtained by criminal groups on the black market.

3. Virtual Methods

This relates to cyber space, which is the Internet. Let us imagine you receive an attached file in an email or a link in one of your social media applications, requesting you to open the attached file or click on the link. If you do so, a malicious virus or worm is downloaded which has the ability to steal all your personal information and pass it on to hackers. We have discussed this in previous chapters. This is a simple way to obtain not only your passwords, but all kinds of personal information stored in your digital devices.

Let us also imagine you access a website to search for information or find out if you can purchase a product, then you are requested to fill out a form or carry out a payment transaction, unaware that this is a fraudulent website. The result will be that all your personal information and financial transactions are copied and stored in the hackers' digital devices.

This is a gold mine for criminal groups. Although such operations require technical hacking skills, they are very simple and are carried out on a daily basis. Loss of identity and fraudulent activity are on the rise. Billions of dollars are made by criminal groups using these methods, more than through any other form of theft.

Many owners of digital devices who use them on a daily basis are unaware of how insecure their personal information is. Although people have become aware of these kinds of theft and fraud, they still fall victim to them. Social media applications have become addictive and there is pressure to respond to friends and people who would like to interact, even if some of these messages are actually from bad actors practicing phishing.

Legal authorities have difficulty identifying such criminal hackers due to the fact that most hacking happens across international borders. Best practice by authorities is to report the incident to their counterparts in other countries, in the hope that the perpetrators will be caught and brought to justice.

The authorities face difficulties in locating these international criminal hackers because of the advanced hacking tools and worms in their arsenals. The list includes spyware, keyloggers, Trojans, backdoors and many others which are highly effective and difficult to remove from digital devices.

PREVENTIVE MEASURES

There are a number of preventive measures users can deploy in their personal digital devices to prevent cyber intrusions. Physical protection measures are simple, i.e. to protect digital devices from loss or misplacement, although there will always be incidents of theft and loss, especially during travel or constant movement between places in a locality.

Users should always be alert to incoming unidentified or suspicious emails or messages with links, even from people who are known and trusted.

If a digital device is behaving in a strange way, such as being slow to react to commands or typing, taking more time to save or retrieve documents, or constantly being interrupted, then it is advisable to scan the device with updated anti-viruses, to clean it from viruses and worms. The biggest causes of concern are the types of worms mentioned above (spyware, Trojans, backdoors and others) which exhibit stealth (hidden) capabilities. They are hard to discover and many anti-viruses commercially available cannot clean them. They require advanced anti-viruses which are typically unaffordable for ordinary users.

Changing passwords is the most common practice to maintain cybersecurity and this should be done frequently, at least every three months. This practice will make it harder for hackers to keep coming back into the digital device and accessing stored applications.

CONCLUSION

Your digital devices are your repository of all your personal information and should be protected by all means. Access to them means that your identity can be compromised and used for fraudulent activities by criminal groups around the world.

Reporting fraud incidents to local authorities can help future prevention of fraud, but by the time you have made the report, it might be too late to prevent damage.

You should be conscious of potential cyberattacks and wary of clicking on links attached to text messages or sent in social media interactions, or of opening files attached to emails. It is simple to launch a virus or worm and, depending on the objective of the attack, your credentials such as passwords will probably be stolen, giving hackers access to your personal information, and possibly leading to sale of your identity to a third party.

CHAPTER 11
Social Engineering

The term social engineering means that a person can manipulate socially available information about a particular person in order to obtain credentials such as login information to be used for further hacking and fraudulent activities. The personal information can be gained off line through one-to-one interactions or from third-parties who share key insights about the person.

There are many well-known cases of famous people who were not necessarily technically smart but managed to obtain certain credentials with little effort and without the technical tools available today.

SMART NON-TECHNICAL

These are people who can acquire the credentials of users by guessing the passwords used to login. They collect as much information as possible about targeted victims, using human skill to manipulate them into releasing information or providing credentials, since they believe that those contacting them are legitimate people.

For example, a clever person can pretend to be an employee and phone the help desk of the IT manager requesting a change of password, using the excuse of not being able to access his account or not remembering the old password. If this person is believable and lucky enough, the manager will give him a temporary password. He will then be able to change the password and access the network system.

Another example is password guessing, using information widely available on social media applications. With the popularity of social media connectivity, users post all kinds of personal information on their applications, whether it is Twitter, Instagram, Facebook or others. Smart hackers can combine alphabetical letters representing login credentials such as user identification and passwords.

Another way to describe social engineering is that it is a non-technical intrusion, relying heavily on human qualities to reveal sensitive and privileged information which compromises standard security procedures. Social engineering can be either human- or computer-based.

Human-based social engineering involves going to the targets and trying to get the maximum information possible about their credentials. People become vulnerable to these kinds of attacks when they carelessly leave behind personal data on social media. Computer-based social engineering is where hackers with technical skills utilize available tools to scan the victim's system and obtain the desired information.

INSIDE JOB ATTACKS

This type of cyberattack is typically performed within the target network system's organization. Inside attacks are orchestrated by employees who are not happy with their jobs and organizations. They have specific grievances or personal grudges and take revenge. Many sophisticated inside jobs are carried out by professional people who have mastered the art of penetrating organizations' sites physically. They are able to plant and insert the required input devices into network systems. Individual inside jobs are easy to discover, and devices used to launch worms easily identified through the machine manufacturing code (MAC), which is the machine identification number. Furthermore, if connected to the Internet, then the IP (Internet Protocol) address can also be located, and the person identified. The exceptions to this are when the inside job is performed on a device connected to the network that does not belong to the attacker.

PHISHING

This is the most common type of hacking. Hackers send phishing emails to hacked accounts with a link that contains a worm to be launched into the victim's computer system. An example is to inform targeted victims that they have won a prize or a lottery, and when they click on a link to register their win or claim their prize, a worm is launched. The victim is then redirected to a web page in which they enter, for example, details of their bank accounts, names, addresses, banks and other personal information.

A Trojan horse is one of the most lethal worms. It is attached to an email, text message or any type of social media application and is launched when the victim opens an attached file or clicks on a link sent to them. Depending on its mission, it will search for particular library files containing vulnerabilities and exploit them. If its purpose is to spy on an intended victim, then it will look in specific libraries that are hidden (stealth).

HACKING USING KALI

Kali is used by many professional and advanced hackers to hack into different computing environments. There are many examples of cyberattacks using Kali and it is used in cybersecurity teaching programs.

Advanced hackers who use Kali to launch cyberattacks know that anti-viruses and firewalls will ultimately prevent the launching of

Kali worms. However, advanced hackers can integrate different worm payloads into Kali tools and techniques and if these worms are new, then hacking can be successful as they will pass through anti-viruses and firewalls.

Kali is a hacking language that can be downloaded publicly and installed into the hacker's system. There are built-in tools and techniques in Kali, but hackers will also use other third-party tools and techniques, in addition to viruses and worms.

The following are some of the tools and techniques used by hackers.

THE SOCIAL ENGINEERING TOOLKIT (SET) IN KALI

Hacking languages such as Kali or Python have a set of tools that hackers can use to launch their viruses and worms. These tools require a certain level of technical skill and mastery of Linux commands, but they are not hard to learn if the proper steps are followed.

SET in Kali is a menu-driven attack system that mainly concentrates on attacking human elements of security. There are a wide variety of attacks available. It is essential to own and use this toolkit for penetration testing. SET comes pre-installed in Kali Linux.

The following screenshot displays the SET toolkit menu:

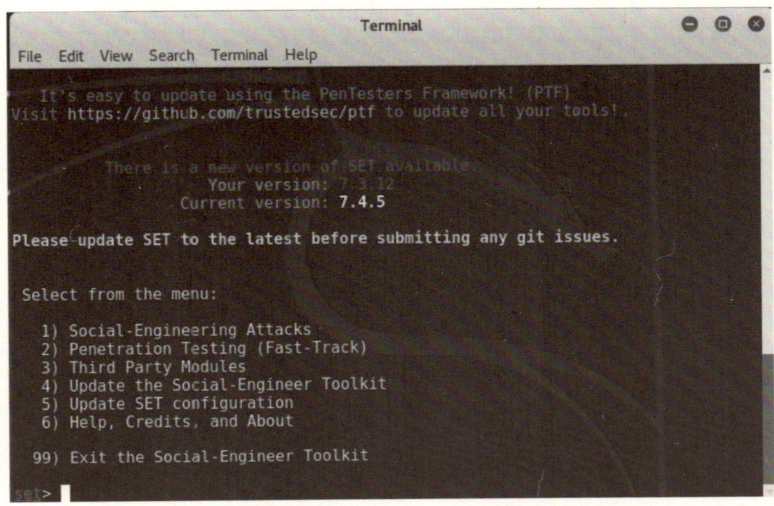

CONCLUSION

There are many ways to practice social engineering in order to acquire victims' credentials. Some of them rely on human intelligence rather than technical skill, while others are technically advanced methods using tools and techniques such as Kali Linus.

The objective is to be able to acquire credentials to access users' accounts and exploit the information there for fraudulent, criminal activities. Criminal groups all over the world use the Internet as a platform to trap the owners of digital devices into revealing sensitive information and credentials, causing serious financial and personal harm, which may be permanent.

There are many steps which can be taken to minimize such activities, including password protection measures and having an increased awareness that any emails or text messages with links should be studied very carefully, regardless of their origins, as they may be attempts at phishing. Furthermore, anti-viruses, firewalls and other tools and software systems can be employed to minimize the threats of incoming Internet traffic and websites infected with viruses and worms.

CHAPTER 12

Backup and Recovery

Data backup and recovery is a process whereby online transactions conducted by users connected to a network system are stored in mass storage devices, such as servers used by the iCloud. These devices are different, depending on whether the user is online or offline when the data is backed up.

Recovery is the process of recovering from online storage devices all the data lost or altered, either by mistake or intentionally. Recovery can be from either online or offline storage devices.

WHY IS BACKUP NEEDED?

This process of backing-up your data is essential when you are dealing with computers and digital devices which store all types of data, including documents, files, pictures, multi-media content or other data communications such as text and social interactions. The process is often ignored by individuals, but from a business point of view it is essential and cannot be ignored.

For many users of portable devices such as mobile phones, iPads, laptops and any other devices which can store information in their hard disks (storage chips), the backup process is mostly ignored and not set up regularly. Most portable devices provide backup services if activated in "setup" to back up at a determined time into the cloud storage provided either by manufacturers of the devices or other applications and companies, for a fee.

THE DANGER OF NO BACKUP

If we assume that an owner of a digital portable device such as a mobile phone with a minimum 64 GB (Gigabytes) of storage data has not backed up the phone data into another digital device or in the cloud, the consequences of the phone being lost, stolen or corrupted will be catastrophic. The user will be unable to recover the addresses of relatives, friends and business associates, along with pictures, videos, text messages and all kinds of valuable information. It may be that information gathered over a couple of years will have vanished forever. Therefore, it is highly recommended that a backup process is activated regularly and multiple storage devices used in order to ensure recovery of data when needed. Recent global surveys found that over 40% of individuals do not back up their data, despite the fact that over 70% are aware of the serious consequences of losing it.

DISASTER RECOVERY

Disaster recovery is a method used by an organization to regain access and restore functionality to its IT infrastructure after a natural or human disaster.

Natural disasters may include fire, earthquakes, floods and wars. Human disasters refer to actions taken by human beings and include errors, damage, sabotage, hardware failures and data breaches due to hacking.

Many businesses, especially companies providing essential services such as airlines, hotels, oil and gas companies, transport companies and others maintaining infrastructures have disaster backup and recovery sites. These sites are typically connected online with the main computing centers of the business enterprises.

For individuals, a disaster refers to the loss of a portable device such as a mobile phone, irreversible damage to stored data, or hacking and ransoming the device, disabling access to stored data.

Individual owners of digital portable devices have similar disaster recovery sites, either in portable units such as Flash USBs, Zip storage units, or in the cloud.

The recovery process is similar for both businesses and individual owners of portable devices. When a disaster occurs, data is recovered from backup storage and restored to the businesses' computers or individual devices.

DATA BREACH

We have discussed this issue in previous chapters.

A data breach refers to an action taken by bad actors, specifically hackers, with criminal intent to steal records and data stored in devices owned by individuals or businesses.

Personal digital devices and enterprises across the globe have witnessed data breaches through hacking, using malicious viruses and worms. These are disasters and the recovery process is activated to recover as much compromised data as possible from the backup system, if stored data has been damaged or access of authorized users has been blocked.

Ransomware called crypto ransomware has been used to deny access to authorized users. When this worm is downloaded into a digital device, it encrypts all the stored data and access is denied to owners of the device unless a ransom is paid, using crypto currency. When payment is made, a code is sent by the hacker to the user, who enters it in order to decrypt the data.

However, if the user has no backup and refuses to pay the ransom, the digital device can be considered dead and all the data lost. Backup is therefore necessary to protect the device in the event of a ransomware disaster. This backup and recovery system is highly recommended by cybersecurity specialists. The practice of backup and recovery is increasingly popular, and awareness of its importance has been heightened due to the increase in hacking activities by international criminal groups.

RECOMMENDED PROTECTION MEASURES

The following are the minimum protection measures which can be taken to protect digital devices from loss of data in the event of disasters.

1. Always practice backup of all data stored in digital devices.
2. Backup must be carried out regularly and backup devices stored in safe places.
3. If backup units are not available, there is always cloud storage backup supplied by companies and manufacturers of digital devices.
4. Ensure digital device software and applications are updated to reduce discovered vulnerability and hacking by bad actors.
5. Passwords must be changed on a regular basis to reduce hacking and minimize risk.
6. Use anti-viruses and intrusion detection systems to block viruses and worms from downloading into digital devices.
7. Be wary of opening files attached to emails or clicking on links showing in text messages from unknown senders. Also, question unusual mails and texts coming from known senders.

CONCLUSION

The backup and recovery process is critical in order to protect data stored in digital devices. Unfortunately, given the huge numbers of portable devices and lack of awareness of many users, it is frequently not practiced and therefore the loss of personal data of individuals is on the rise. For businesses, the practice of backup and recovery is commonly practiced and considered a must.

Currently, advanced hackers using the latest hacking tools and techniques are able to breach data in all types of businesses and in individual portable digital devices almost on a daily basis. Criminal groups have realized that it is easier and more profitable to use stolen personal data for identity theft, making millions of dollars, than robbing a bank physically in broad daylight.

Backup and recovery will ease the pain for many enterprises and owners of digital devices who need to recover stolen data. Recovery is possible when backup exists.

CHAPTER 13

Cyber Warfare vs. Electronic Warfare

There are differences between cyber warfare and electronic warfare. When it comes to military operations, dependence on electronic warfare is overwhelming and started early in the 20th century.

Cyber warfare developed recently as an important element in military operations, complementing electronic warfare. As time goes on, it plays an increasingly significant role in military operations. Although differences between the two remain, experts in electronic warfare are now recruiting cyber warfare specialists to work alongside them.

In the modern world, military operations depend on an electromagnetic spectrum. The military use cyberspace to communicate, gather intelligence and carry out surveillance which is defensive or facilitates attacks on enemies' locations and equipment.

Before looking at the major differences, it is important to have a definition of each term.

Electronic Warfare (EW) operations involve the control and dominance of the electronic spectrum. This means being able to control different types of radio frequencies of the enemy, gaining a military advantage. The dependency of armies on two-way radio communication (EMS) has been the main pillar of military operations.

The Department of Defense defined EMS radio communication as the following:

1. Radio communications to communicate with different allied (friendly) forces in the battlefield.

2. Application of different radio communications involving various technologies, such as microwaves, data links, radar and satellite communications.
3. The use of infrared in targeting enemy locations.
4. Application of laser technologies to transmit data and destroy targets.

Therefore, EMS involves three types: electronic protection, electronic attacks and electronic warfare support. Three teams specializing in these areas are part of the military electronic warfare department.

Cyber warfare operations involve the use of the latest military technology to deliver malicious codes to enemy networks, using cyberspace and radio frequency (wireless) systems. The goal is to destroy, spy on or disable these networks.

The following Table displays the differences between the two forms of warfare.

Cyber Warfare vs. Electronic Warfare

	Electronic Warfare	Cyber Warfare
Mission	• Air situation picture (surveillance) • Guiding missiles • Navigation • C&C/data networks	• IT • SCADA • Business • Government services
Intelligence	• SIGINT (ELINT, COMINT) • IMINT (Opt., Radar)	• Hacking • Accessibility tools

Attack	• Electronic Attack (EA)
	  • ECM (Victim: radars)
	  • ComJam (Victim: comm. links)
		• Cyber attacks
		  • (Victim: network services & resources)

Attack type	• Jamming
	  • Spoofing, noise
	• Deception
	  • False targets, missile stealing
		• Jamming
		  • DoS, DDoS
		• Deception
		  • Identity theft, MITM, phishing, Trojan horses

Counter-measures	• ECCM:
	  • Filters, guards, SLB&SLC
	  • Decoys
	• Immunity
	  • LPI: waveform, agility
		• Counter-measures
		  • FW, IPS
		  • Honeypots
		• Immunity
		  • Encryption, virtualization

IAI 4 RSACONFERENCE2014

THE ADVANTAGE OF CYBER WARFARE

The biggest advantage of cyber warfare happening alongside electronic warfare is that malicious codes can be delivered to closed networks. Closed networks are networks not connected to the Internet.

Malicious codes can be sent to the enemy's networks using radio frequencies, and new technologies of jamming can turn off all electronic equipment within a radius of 3.5 km.

There are a number of advanced military aircraft equipped with jamming, spying and electronic delivery systems. They can fly at the highest levels in space, or low levels in silence mode (stealth), avoiding radar detection. They are extremely expensive and designed to certain specifications for each country's air force, possessing defensive or offensive capabilities or both.

The country that controls the space above earth through satellites has a big advantage in cyber warfare. Satellite communications depend on radio frequencies coming from earth. Current technology allows us to communicate with satellites 400 miles above earth, commanding them to transmit communication and deliver cyber weapons if needed.

It is notable that new fighter aircraft are equipped with cyber capabilities that penetrate enemy networks. The F-35 and F-22 are equipped with communications to impact electrotactic signals of the enemy without being detected or intercepted. The delivery of malicious codes is also potentially possible, although such capabilities are not yet reported for these fighters. However, it would not be surprising if such capabilities exist.

In 2010, the Department of Defense (DOD) of the United States of America designated cyberspace as the fifth global fighting domain after land, sea, air and space, since anyone who controls the information environment can affect the outcome of wars. The ability to limit or completely block the enemy's access to information, therefore limiting their situational awareness, can and will change outcomes.

Due to the importance of cyberwarfare, the DOD has established the U.S. Cyber Command. In addition, another department called "Cyberspace Electronic" was set up when electronic warfare was merged with cyber warfare. There is a high level of coordination between this department and the Cyber Command. The mission of both is to utilize applications and technologies to enable the military to defend themselves and to deter, detect and attack enemies in cyberspace.

CHAPTER 14
The Chinese Model

Qatar is an Arabian Gulf country. It has a small population with one of the highest Internet penetration rates.

Senior officials in Qatar and its sister GCC countries pride themselves on the technological advancement of their societies and they have made it a national policy to promote e-government platforms across all state entities. They even encourage important private industries such as banks, transport, oil and gas companies to join in this open Internet environment and connect to e-government platforms.

Here comes the big question. Although it is a source of pride to have a high penetration of Internet and connectivity in such a small country, Qatar must be able to safeguard its vital sectors against cyberattacks. Senior officials say they are doing their best to protect the country, but there is a greater risk of cyber threats, due to high Internet penetration and mobility.

These officials admit they will not be able to stop cyberattacks and damage caused by hackers, but they claim that this is a tradeoff for an open Internet society and that it is impossible to stop cyberattacks. What is the solution? Here, let us introduce the Chinese model of a cyber command center, which so far has been successfully applied in a nation of 1.5 billion.

If it can be done for a country with the largest population in the world, then it can be done for countries with smaller populations like Qatar and GCC nations. The Chinese model is based on a single principle, which is to stop any cyber intruder entering its cyberspace.

At the same time, China has not lost the benefits of the Internet and has created a knowledge-based economy which is now the second largest in the world after the United States. It retains central control over three main areas within the information and communication technology sector.

We will notice three characteristics of the Chinese model.

OBJECTIVE

First, China had to establish firm control over the Internet and control the types of software used in the country. Facebook, Twitter and other Western-developed social media are not permitted to operate in the country; they are blocked. It is only possible to use social media created by local Chinese companies. In this way, the government controls and monitors all traffic moving in and out of these social media systems using the Internet.

TELECOM COMPANIES

Second, China has its own telecommunication companies that are under the control of the Chinese government, although some of them are privatized and their shares traded locally on the stock market. However, they are still maintained and controlled by the government.

Therefore, all ISPs Tier 1 and other traffic use fiber optics across, in and out of the country, and these are linked with international fiber optic cables.

All traffic is under the control of the military Cyber Command and Control Center. This center has the local intrusion and detection programs necessary to stop intruders entering the country.

Third, and most importantly, hardware and software systems used by vital industries and companies within China and for Chinese government agencies must abide by the security regulations of the country.

THE SOURCE CODE

What does this mean? All foreign hardware and software sold within China must be inspected and the source codes handed over for certification and approval. This allows the Chinese government to modify the source code of any software and have it approved for use within China.

This was the reason for the delay in introducing the new Apple iPhone into China. The phone has a security feature and therefore the Chinese government insisted that unless Apple released the source code of this feature to the Chinese government, Apple iPhone would not be sold in China, which is one of the largest single markets for Apple phones. After six months of negotiation, Apple agreed to the Chinese government's demand.

DISCOVERING WEAKNESSES

If there are any weaknesses or gaps within software systems, such as the zero-day weakness found in many operating systems and applications sold worldwide by major software and hardware companies, then China will discover and eliminate it.

The government is aware that if a hacker discovers such weaknesses, he or she will take advantage of them and hack into the system. Therefore, the Chinese government certifies the products of foreign technology companies before they can operate and sell their products in China.

GOVERNMENT REGULATIONS

Apple's phone components are made in China and it considers China its biggest outsource market outside the United States. China has drafted government regulations forcing all hardware and software technology vendors to abide by very strict security guidelines before they enter the Chinese market and start selling either to government or private entities. Microsoft Windows found themselves in a similar situation to Apple many years ago. China is a huge market for technology companies. If they are not in China, their market share will not be as good.

WHY DO THE CHINESE DO IT?

The objective is twofold. One is to ensure the maintenance of national security, preventing cyber spying or cyber threats which could arise as a result of having foreign technologies on their soil. Second, China aims to reduce reliance on foreign technologies, and to encourage and promote sales and innovation of locally manufactured Chinese technologies.

THE REACTION OF FOREIGN COMPANIES

The initial reaction of many Western companies who had been operating and selling their products in China for a long time was negative. They complained to the Chinese authorities and urged Beijing to review existing regulations, without success. Following Edward Snowden's disclosure of the USA's surveillance, using various viruses and worms embedded in Western hardware and software, the Chinese government has become even more paranoid.

THE CHINESE POSITION

The Chinese position with regards to its regulations and dealings with Western companies has been reinforced and these companies have to live with the fact that their know-how and intellectual property must be handed over to Chinese regulators before any sale or operation can take place within the country.

The Chinese Banking Regulatory Commission has issued strict and lengthy regulations, describing security measures for technology companies selling to all banks in China, local or foreign.

TECHNOLOGICAL PRODUCTS

Chinese regulations cover many different technological products, such as PCs, servers, routers, wireless products, ATM machines and many others. They also demand that source codes for all types of software including databases, operating systems, middleware, virtual private networks and others are registered with the government and obtain security clearance and certification.

Companies such as IBM, EMC, Microsoft and Hewlett-Packard have been operating in China for a long time and they have large numbers of customers in the business and financial sectors, mainly banks.

INTELLECTUAL PROPERTY

The release of the source codes of different hardware or software products have made American and European companies nervous. Many of them refuse to oblige, since the release of source codes means the loss of intellectual property. These companies have spent so much money on research and development and are afraid the Chinese will pass on the source codes to their local manufacturers. It is then only a matter of time before they are copied and sold, creating competition and threatening foreign companies' market share and dominance, which they have long enjoyed.

Many companies have sold their business in China to Chinese companies in order not to have to abide by these strict security regulations.

REFUSAL TO FOLLOW REGULATION

HP's decision to sell its Chinese networking unit attracted many potential bidders in China. The expectation is that other companies will follow suit. Since China is the second largest consumer market after the United States, many American and European companies may have to compromise by submitting their source codes in order to be able to operate in the country. Foreign companies which do not meet government guidelines will be banned from selling their products in China, especially to government entities and government-owned companies. An example is the Microsoft Windows 8.1 operating system.

THE IMPORTANCE OF NATIONAL SECURITY

Many foreign companies have caved in and cooperated with the Chinese government, revealing their source codes and other vital security measures within their products. This helps China protect its vital infrastructure from potential cyberattacks. National security is more important to the government than having foreign companies operating and selling in China. In addition, the Chinese government aims to use this tactic to promote local Chinese companies, which are able to sell their products to government entities and increase their market share. Many such companies developing advanced technology products have become as good as their American and European counterparts and sell well within China and internationally. Companies such Huawei, Inspur Group Ltd. and ZTE are among the biggest Chinese companies operating internationally, exporting computing and telecommunication products.

THE GREAT FIREWALL

China created the great firewall to protect its country. This is similar to the Great Wall of China, built to protect major Chinese cities against invaders, which became one of the wonders of the world. China's firewall screens every outgoing and incoming electronic transmission and provides the necessary protection against potential cyber threats from malware and viruses coming into the country.

One of the main difficulties in implementing this Chinese model for Qatar and the other GCC countries is that these countries rely heavily on automation and networking in connecting their vital infrastructure to the Internet, thus making them susceptible to cyberattacks.

CHINA'S LEVEL OF DEVELOPMENT

China uses less computerized automation, which makes it worry less about hacking. It considers itself to be a developed country similar to Qatar and other GCC countries.

This is not exactly true, as China is not considered as advanced as Western countries, Japan and Korea in the adaptation of automation in critical systems such as power grids and machines controlled by computers.

THE CLOSED INTERNET

Much of the country's major infrastructure still relies on manual controls. In order to provide it with automation to compete internationally and reduce overall costs, closed Internet (which is called intranet) is sometimes utilized.

This means that a company's private Internet is not open to the worldwide Internet, but automation is supplied through a closed circuit. The company is connected to the national Internet in a strictly controlled way.

ECONOMIC POWER

China has the second highest GDP in the world, after the United States. The country is so reliant on exports of its various products and technologies that automation is inevitable. But its greatest advantage, as already stated, is the state's control of the Internet, which cascades into various intranets of state-owned enterprises and other companies operating under the control of the Communist party. Open Internet societies offer a tradeoff between wide access to information for their citizens and threats of cyberattacks which can endanger the economic interests of entities operating in the country.

DEFENSIVE CAPABILITIES

It is important to realize that any defense against cyberattacks in a highly automated society is going to be weak, given recent advances in hacking knowledge and technology. The belief that highly automated and connected nations have strong cyber national policies and effective measures to protect vital sectors of their economy from cyberattacks is no longer grounded in reality.

CHINA'S POLICY – POTENTIAL HACKING

Many nations speak of having national firewalls, strong intrusion detection and powerful anti-virus programs, making it hard for a hacker to penetrate their systems, but there is always the inside job: hacking by individuals or groups of people from the inside, with different motivations.

Despite China's policy with regards to the Internet, its strict regulations on the use of hardware and software and its centralized cyber command and control over a vast country with the biggest population on earth, hacking still takes place. However, hacking into China from the outside is likely to require advanced skills and technology only possessed by nations such as the United States. The majority of hacking attacks in the country, which are never reported due to information and press control, are inside jobs. When an inside hacking job occurs and a virus or worm is discovered, it is immediately contained within the attacked entity, since Internet connection between entities in China is highly restricted and controlled. Virus mutation to another entity or computing system is eliminated on the spot.

THE DIFFICULTY OF HACKING INTO CHINA

The difficulty of hacking into China stems from the fact that existing hacking takes advantage of zero time or date types of applications in EXE files of operating systems. All such applications and operating systems in China have already been cleansed and any weaknesses eliminated under existing regulations.

NATIONAL CYBER SCORE

In his recent book, *Cyber War: The Next Threat To National Security And What To Do About It*, Richard Clarke designed a table with scores giving the dependency ranking of nations on automation and their susceptibility to cyberattacks.

China has the second highest defense ranking after North Korea. Clarke states that China could disconnect itself from the rest of the world and thereby totally isolate itself from cyber threats. North Korea is ranked number one because of its limited Internet usage and limited or non-existent automation in the critical sectors of its economy, where operations are typically done manually, thereby making the nation less susceptible to cyber threats coming from outside or even inside the country.

INTRANET SYSTEM

The fact that major infrastructure in China and North Korea is less dependent on automation is not the key issue. The main issue is that when companies operate in vital sectors of the economy, they use a closed intranet system within a highly secured environment. If there is a requirement or need to be connected to each other or to the Internet, this connection is controlled and overseen by the Cyber Command and Control Center in order to maintain cybersecurity.

THE ADOPTION OF THE CHINESE MODEL

Many countries avoid the adoption of the Chinese Model as it is extremely restrictive and can only function in an authoritarian and controlled environment. In addition, China is so technologically advanced that it has been able to substitute Western technologies with local ones, giving them similar and, in many cases, better capabilities. The Internet is widely available in China, but Chinese citizens and visitors to the country use Chinese Internet portals and companies to connect to the outside world. However, as stated, a few Western technology companies are permitted to operate in the country, as long as they are certified by Chinese government entities.

CONCLUSION AND TAKEAWAYS

This book has been written in order to simplify the concept of cybersecurity and provide people with the tools to understand the issue in a larger context, while also providing understanding on how it can affect our everyday lives.

The term cybersecurity itself has been defined, along with the various terminologies relating to it. Readers have been provided with the historical context of cybersecurity and information about incidents that have occurred in various parts of the world and how they were dealt with. Additionally, they have been provided with knowledge and information about how to avoid cybersecurity threats.

Key takeaways to keep in mind when approaching the issue of cybersecurity include:

- Understanding the various risks of being connected to the Internet, given the widespread use of different types of social media applications and business applications that employ a wide variety of data collection software to invade users' privacy.
- Understanding the importance of privacy and the protection of personal information and various forms of data representing one's identity.
- The world's dependency on the Internet and wireless communications has created risk for users and opportunities for individuals and groups of criminals who can exploit various vulnerabilities in the hardware and software applications we constantly use and operate.

- Such vulnerabilities enable criminals to hack and steal valuable personal data stored online and transmitted across the Internet.
- The process of keeping your data secure through backup in separate storage locations and devices can also pose cybersecurity threats, but it is an essential preventive measure, in case of technological malfunction and crisis.
- The Chinese model offers a better protective approach to nations and various organizations whose online operations are highly mission critical.
- The Chinese model is not for every country, especially those countries which are industrial, democratic and economically diversified, but it may be suitable for state-controlled nations interested in obtaining maximum cybersecurity.

REFERENCES

Al-Dorani, Mohammed (2015) *Cyber Danger, GCC Countries & Qatar*. CreateSpace Independent Publishing Platform.

Al-Dorani, Mohammed (2019) *Cyber War: Qatar Blockade - GCC Countries*. Independently published.

Aukta, Shikha (2019) '10 Types of Hackers You Should Know', 13 June.

Buchanan, Ben (2017) 'The Cybersecurity Dilemma: Where Thucydides Meets Cyberspace', *Harvard Kennedy School Belfer Center for Science and International Affairs, Council on Foreign Relations*, https://www.cfr.org/blog/cybersecurity-dilemma-where-thucydides-meets-cyberspace. 30 January.

Chabrow, Eric (2012) 'Aligning Electronic and Cyber Warfare: Similarities Exist between the Two, but They Are Not the Same', *Gov Info Security*, 10 July.

Clark, Patrick (2018) 'Marriott Breach Exposes Weakness in Cyber Defenses for Hotels', *Bloomberg*, 14 December. https://www.bloomberg.com/news/articles/2018-12-14/marriott-cyber-breach-shows-industry-s-hospitality-to-hackers.

Congressional Research Service (2019) 'Convergence of Cyberspace Operations and Electronic Warfare', *IN FOCUS*, 13 August.

Course Hero, "Authentication is the process ensuring that", Texas A&M University, 2021.

Document Solutions, Inc (2019) 'IT Disaster Recovery: What Happens After a Data Breach?', 6 May. blog.dsinm.com/blog/it-disaster-recovery-what-happens-after-a-data-breach.

Federal Trade Commission (2020) 'Equifax Data Breach Settlement', January. https://www.ftc.gov/enforcement/cases-proceedings/refunds/equifax-data-breach-settlement.

Finkle, Jim and Dhanya Skariachan (2013) 'Target cyber breach hits 40 million payment cards at holiday peak', *Reuters*, 19 December. https://www.reuters.com/article/us-target-breach-idUSBRE9BH1GX20131219.

Fleishman, Glenn (2018) 'Equifax Data Breach, One Year Later: Obvious Errors and No Real Changes, New Report says', *FORTUNE*, 8 September. https://fortune.com/2018/09/07/equifax-data-breach-one-year-anniversary/.

Global Knowledge (2021) "Cybersecurity Glossary of Terms". https://www.globalknowledge.com/us-en/topics/cybersecurity/glossary-of-terms/.

Hoogenraad, Wim (2019) 'The Internet of Things and 6 major security problems', *ITpedia*, 1 February. https://en.itpedia.nl/2019/02/01/het-internet-of-things-en-6-grote-security-problemen/.

Kan, Michael (2017) 'Yahoo execs botched its response to 2014 breach, investigation finds', *CSO, United Kingdom*, 2 March. https://www.csoonline.com/article/3176181/yahoo-execs-botched-its-response-to-2014-breach-investigation-finds.html.

Kello, Lucas (2017) 'The Security Dilemma of Cyber Space: Ancient Logic, New Problems', *LAWFARE*, 28 August.

Libicki, Martin C. (2016) *Jstor* and (2018) 'Is There a Cybersecurity Dilemma?', *The Cyber Defense Review* 1(1): 129-140. https://www.jstor.org/stable/26267303?seq=2#metadata_info_tab_contents. https://www.google.com/search?q=internet+security+dilemma&oq=internet+security+dilemma&aqs=chrome..69i57.12779j1j4&sourceid=chrome&ie=UTF-8.

Locker, Melissa (2019) 'A Telegram chat may (rightfully) bring down Puerto Rico's governor', *FAST COMPANY*, 16 July. https://www.fastcompany.com/90377221/a-telegram-chat-may-rightfully-bring-down-puerto-ricos-governor.

Lord, Nate (2018) 'What is Email Security? Data Protection 101', *DIGITAL GUARDIAN, DATAINSIDER*, 11 September.

https://digitalguardian.com/blog/what-email-security-data-protection-101.

Milkovic, Deon (2020) '25 Cyber Security Terms That Everyone Who Uses A Computer Should Know', *Cybint*, 23 July. https://www.cybintsolutions.com/16-cyber-security-terms-that-you-should-know/.

Nachreiner, Corey (2017) 'Will 2017 be the year of Ransomware', *Help Net Security*, 10 January. https://www.helpnetsecurity.com/2017/01/10/ransomworm/.

Ng, Alfred (2018) 'Equifax's data breach by the numbers: The full breakdown', *CNET*, 8 May. https://www.cnet.com/news/equifaxs-data-breach-by-the-numbers-the-full-breakdown/.

Nohe, Patrick (2018) 'Five ways to determine if a Website is Fake, Fraudulent, or a Scam – 2018", *hashedout by The SSL Store*, 2 November.https://www.thesslstore.com/blog/5-ways-to-determine-if-a-website-is-fake-fraudulent-or-a-scam/.

O'Flaherty, Kate (2018) 'Marriott Breach - - What Happened, How Serious Is It And Who Is Impacted?', *Forbes*, 30 November. https://www.forbes.com/sites/kateoflahertyuk/2018/11/30/marriott-breach-what-happened-how-serious-is-it-and-who-is-impacted/#2c0cf7f67d25.

Oprysko, Caitlin (2019) 'Fox News anchor shreds Puerto Rican governor over salacious messages', *POLITICO*, 22 July. https://www.politico.com/story/2019/07/22/fox-puerto-rico-governor-rossello-1426455.

Outpost24 (2018) 'Top 10 of the world's largest cyberattacks, and how to prevent them', 3 December. https://outpost24.com/blog/top-10-of-the-world-biggest-cyberattacks.

Prior, Ryan (2019) 'Equifax will pay up to 700 million over its data breach. Here's how to claim your money', *CNN BUSINESS*, 26 July. https://www.cnn.com/2019/07/25/us/equifax-700-million-settlement-data-breach-trnd/index.html.

Profis, Sharon (2017) 'Equifax data breach: Find out if you were one of 143 million hacked', *CNET*, 11 September. https://www.cnet.com/how-to/equifax-data-breach-find-out-if-you-were-one-of-143-million-hacked/.

Rosencrance, Linda and Madelyn Bacon (2021) 'What is social engineering?', *TechTarget. SearchSecurity*. June. https://searchsecurity.techtarget.com/definition/social-engineering.

Seth, Preeti (2019) '40 Most Common Cyber Security Terms That Everyone Should Know', *TWEAK Library*, 19 August. https://tweaklibrary.com/40-cyber-security-terms-you-should-be-knowing/.

Singha, Rajiv (2018) 'THE A-Z DICTIONARY OF CYBERSECURITY TERMS', *Quick Heal Blog, Security Simplified*, 15 March. https://blogs.quickheal.com/the-a-z-dictionary-of-cybersecurity-terms/.

Schwartz, Mathew J. (2016) 'Yahoo Hacked by Cybercrime Gangs, Security Firm Reports', BANK INFO SECURITY, 29 September.https://www.bankinfosecurity.com/yahoo-hacked-by-cybercrime-gang-security-firm-reports-a-9428.

Sweet, Ken and Michael Liedtke (2017) 'Equifax traced the source of its massive hack to preventable software flaw', *AP (Associated Press)*, 15 September. https://www.businessinsider.com/how-did-equifax-get-hacked-2017-9.

Symposium Eight (2014) 'Countering Asymmetric Threats, A National Imperative: Cyber Electronic Warfare And Critical Infrastructure, Strategies for National Security'. Report on the Eighth Symposium in the Asymmetric Threats to National Security series.

Tan, Huileng (2019) 'Marriott cyberattack traced to Chinese intelligence-gathering effort: NYT', *CNBC*, 11 December. https://www.cnbc.com/2018/12/12/marriot-cyberattack-traced-to-chinese-intelligence-nyt.html.

Tani, Hirashi and Dai Shimogaito 'Disaster Data Recovery'. https://disaster-data-recovery.com/.

Techopedia (2021) 'Internet Security'. https://www.techopedia.com/definition/23548/internet-security.

Techopedia (2021) 'Backup and Recovery'. https://www.techopedia.com/definition/24058/backup-and-recovery.

Theilman, Sam (2016) 'Yahoo hack: 1bn accounts compromised by biggest data breach in history', *The Guardian*, 15 December. https://www.theguardian.com/technology/2016/dec/14/yahoo-hack-security-of-one-billion-accounts-breached.

Wattles, Jackie and Selena Larson (2017) 'How the Equifax data breach happened: What we know now', *CNN BUSINESS*, 16 September. https://money.cnn.com/2017/09/16/technology/equifax-breach-security-hole/index.html.

WIKIPEDIA (2021) 'Equifaxt', 19 June. https://en.wikipedia.org/wiki/Equifax.

WIKIPEDIA (2021) 'Browser security', 7 May. https://en.wikipedia.org/wiki/Browser_security.

Wroclawski, Daniel (2019) 'How to Keep Your Home Security Cameras From Being Hacked', *CR Consumer Reports*, 7 August. https://a.msn.com/r/2/AAFu5xk?m=en-us&ocid=News.